THIS IS
A BOOK
ABOUT
DUMPLINGS

味道

THIS IS A BOOK ABOUT DUMPLINGS

味道

BRENDAN PANG, Founder of Bumplings Perth

PAGE STREET PUBLISHING CO.

PAGE STREET
PUBLISHING CO.

Copyright © 2020 Brendan Pang

First published in 2020 by
Page Street Publishing Co.
27 Congress Street, Suite 105
Salem, MA 01970
www.pagestreetpublishing.com

Distributed by Macmillan, sales in Canada by The Canadian Manda Group.

24   23   22   21   8

ISBN-13: 978-1-64567-034-6
ISBN-10: 1-64567-034-1

Library of Congress Control Number: 2019951522

Cover and book design by Kylie Alexander for Page Street Publishing Co.

Photography by Thomas Davidson
Illustrations and Brand Design by Ryan Vincent

Printed and bound in the United States

DEDICATION

I would like to acknowledge the Whadjuk Noongar people past, present and future for this book. The ideas, recipes and food within were created on their land.

I'd like to dedicate this book to my Grandmère. If she hadn't been so excited about cooking herself, sharing her knowledge and exposing me to different foods, I wouldn't be where I am today.

From a young age, I didn't have much of an appetite—I would rather have played—but she forced me to eat and eat every last spoonful. Boy, how things have changed!

CONTENTS

General Introduction   8

ONE: STEAMED DUMPLINGS   10
Pork and Shrimp Siu Mai   12
Crystal Shrimp Har Gow   15
Swiss Chard and Spinach Jiaozi   16
Scallop and Ginger Dumplings   19
Pork and Peanut Dumplings   20
Shanghai Soup Dumplings   23
Northern-Style Lamb Dumplings   24
Tofu and Kimchi Jiaozi   27

TWO: BOILED DUMPLINGS   28
Spicy Sichuan Pork Wontons   30
Chicken and Ginger Jiaozi   33
Pork and Garlic Chive Jiaozi   34
Lobster XO Dumplings   37
Kang Kung and Tofu Dumplings   38
Red Curry Chicken Wonton Soup   41
Beef Dumplings in Hot and Sour Soup   42
Cantonese-Style Shrimp Wonton Soup   45

THREE: FRIED DUMPLINGS   46
Juicy Chicken Sheng Jian Bao   48
Panfried Chicken and Cabbage Dumplings   51
Panfried Pork and Kimchi Dumplings   52
Chinese Spicy Beef Potstickers   55
Grandmère's Fried Shrimp Wontons   56
Fried BBQ Pork Dumplings   59
Crispy Taro Dumplings   60

FOUR: RAINBOW DUMPLINGS   62
Green: Chicken and Cilantro Dumplings   64
Red: Korean Beef Dumplings   67
Pink: Chinese Roast Duck Dumplings   69
Orange: Pork, Carrot and Ginger Baozi   73
Yellow: Curried Beef Dumplings   74
Blue: Chile Mud Crab Dumplings   77
Purple: Miso Roasted Eggplant Potstickers   78
Black: Black Cod and Chive Dumplings   81

FIVE: BUNS, RICE AND NOODLES   82
Fried Chicken Bao Buns   84
Biang Biang Noodles with Spicy Cumin Lamb   87
BBQ Pork Steamed Buns   91
Pork and Garlic Chive Baozi   92
Sticky Rice Wrapped in Lotus Leaf   95
Classic Chinese Fried Rice   96
Special Crab Fried Rice   99
Cantonese Chicken and Salted Fish Fried Rice   100
BBQ Pork and Crispy Wonton Noodles   103
Spicy Dan Dan Noodles   104

SIX: APPETIZERS AND SNACKS   106
Chinese Pickled Radish   108
Smacked Cucumber Salad   111
Sesame Shrimp Toasts   112
Green Onion Pancake   115
Salt and Pepper Silken Tofu   116

Panfried Radish Cake 119
Fried Squid Tentacles 120
Grilled Five-Spice Steak Jianbing 123
Grandmère's Boxing Chicken 124
Tea-Smoked Duck Breast 127

SEVEN: DUMPLING SAUCES 128
Roasted Sichuan Chile Oil 130
Sichuan Chile Dressing 130
Black Vinegar and Tamari 133
Spiced Vinegar Sauce 133
Mum's Fried Garlic and Soy 134
Sweet-and-Sour Sauce 134
Bang Bang Sauce 137
Ginger-Soy Sticky Sauce 137
XO Sauce 138

EIGHT: DUMPLING WRAPPERS 140
Wonton Wrappers 141
Crystal Dumpling Wrappers 141
Dumpling Wrappers 142
Rainbow Dumpling Wrappers 142

NINE: DUMPLING FOLDS AND SHAPES 143
Triangle Shape 144
The Simple Potsticker 145
Half-Moon 146
Crescent Moon 147
Classic Wonton Fold 148
Gold Ingot Shape 149
Soup Dumpling Shape 150

Acknowledgments 151
About the Author 153
Index 154

CHEW 渤晾筒 DIP 渤 SLURP
JRP 渤晾 CHEW
荡吉饺2

GENERAL INTRODUCTION

I first learned the art of making dumplings from my Grandmère. It all started with the wontons. Back when times were a bit tougher, we used to make these with a simple ground pork filling as she did back in Mauritius.

Nearly two decades since then—when I first started making dumplings— I've harnessed many different cuisines and techniques to incorporate into them, making a name for myself with my dumpling kitchen, Bumplings.

It began as a pop-up concept, operating from an Airstream (essentially a trailer) with traditional Chinese dumplings and Sichuan flavors, but with some freedom to experiment and express my creative side, it's really become my food-studio more than a business! It was always a risk, given there's a strong Cantonese food culture in Perth that really knows its cuisine, but the community has been so supportive and certified my dumplings as the real deal.

It won't surprise you that most of the dishes in this book are dumplings. Purely and simply: There's nothing I love to stuff my face with more! I love how versatile they are, how many different flavors there can be, how nearly every cuisine has its own version of dumplings (*mandu*, gyoza, ravioli, pierogi, *momos*, *jiaozi*, etc.) and especially how they're morsel sized, so it's easy to eat a ton of them!

This book has some recipes that aren't exclusively dumplings, but many are classic Chinese dishes or have traditional flavors that go so perfectly with dumplings. Such dishes as Sticky Rice Wrapped in Lotus Leaf (page 95), BBQ Pork Steamed Buns (page 91) and Panfried Radish Cake (page 119) are the perfect accompaniment—dishes that I love to eat with my dumplings.

Other recipes, such as Grilled Five-Spice Steak Jianbing (page 123), Grandmère's Boxing Chicken (page 124) and Biang Biang Noodles with Spicy Cumin Lamb (page 87), are where I get to share with you dishes that are close to my heart: through being an expression of my artistic side, a recipe I've fallen in love with or a traditional dish passed down through my family that I now want to share with you!

My life has been largely split across three very diverse but equally rich cultures: Chinese, Mauritian and Australian. Although I don't speak any dialect of Chinese, I understand and love so much about Chinese food and culture that just can't be taught in classes—and this whole book pays homage to that. Mauritius really just built on my love of food and enjoying it with those I love. Curries, breads, pickles, stir-fried noodles, rougaille— Mauritian food is all about very honest food with very honest people.

During my time in Broome, I threw myself into the indigenous Australia culture of the Yawuru people—and I am so grateful for this opportunity. Most will never get to have the "true" cultural experience I had in Australia, and for me, it was so familiar and so similar to Mauritian family life and values—food, fishing and family. And like my family, Broome people are feeders! And dumplings are the ultimate food to feed people with.

The purpose of my book is to remove the fear of making dumplings from scratch at home—they're actually nowhere near as hard as you may think!

In this book, I break down what a dumpling is made of—the different elements, the filling; cooking methods (which you might favor depending on your confidence in the kitchen or preference); and ways to turn an ordinary dumpling into a pumped-up one just by serving it with the right accompaniments. And no experience with Chinese food or flavors is required to get started!

Really good dumpling wrappers are commercially available if you're feeling worried about making the dough for the first time—play to your strengths and build your confidence slowly!

As you work your way through this book, you'll learn everything about dumplings and other Chinese classics—from making the dough to rolling out the wrappers, to different shapes, fillings, staple sauces and techniques that are translatable to other cuisines for the more adventurous and experienced home cooks! But if you don't treat this book as a tutorial, that's totally fine! All the recipes are great for anyone to make from home—pick one recipe and make it your signature!

ONE

STEAMED DUMPLINGS

Steamed dumplings are some of my favorite things to eat for dim sum. Just the mention of them makes my mouth water, and on top of being incredibly delicious, there's something very special about sharing these little pockets of joy with those around you. In my family, our usual Sunday brunch at the local *yum cha* house does not go without my cousins and me fighting over the last dumpling in the bamboo steamer, our solution of course being to order more!

The best thing about steamed dumplings is that anyone can make them. There is a common misconception that it requires years of experience to be able to craft a dumpling from scratch, but when broken down into the basics, all you need is flour, water and a tasty filling that, you'll be surprised to learn, can be made from ingredients that are most likely already sitting in your fridge or pantry at home. From vegetables to leftover meat, dumplings can be filled with almost anything.

And if that wasn't enough to lure you into having a crack at making these delectable treats yourself, the simplicity of it all translates into the few utensils and equipment required. At the very most, you may need to purchase a bamboo steamer, which can be found at most Asian supermarkets and specialty food stores. A stand mixer will certainly simplify the process of making dough; however, it is not necessary. Your hands and a rolling pin will do just fine.

When it comes to cooking, ensure your steamer is up and running ten to fifteen minutes before you want to steam your dumplings. Remember, dumplings do not take long to cook and are best eaten immediately to avoid any dryness. An indication of doneness is when the dough has turned translucent and the filling has firmed up. The steaming method guarantees a delicate finish and helps preserve not only the intricate and elegant shapes of the dumplings, but the subtle textures and flavors, too.

Steaming requires more finesse than the other dumpling styles, but this is my favorite way to prepare dumplings and the most familiar for those exposed to traditional Chinese dumplings. I think if you can make any of the recipes from this chapter with pride, you're well equipped to handle the whole book. From making your own dumpling wrappers to mastering traditional fillings and folds, you will soon be proficient with all the necessary tools for making classic and popular dim sum dishes, such as *siu mai* and *har gow*, to mouthwatering soup dumplings.

PORK AND SHRIMP SIU MAI

Siu mai, meaning "cook and sell," are open-topped dumplings filled with a mixture of ground pork and chunks of succulent fresh shrimp. Considered an essential part of the Cantonese dim sum repertoire, siu mai are not only impressive in looks with their golden frilly edges, but also easy to make as a novice cook starting out in the dumpling world.

Unlike most steamed dumplings, the wrapper on a siu mai is made from thin wonton pastry, and although best when made fresh, can also be purchased premade at most Asian grocers. The key to a good siu mai is a firm springy texture that can be achieved using a ratio of 80 percent pork meat to 20 percent pork fat.

MAKES 35 DUMPLINGS

Filling

3 dried shiitake mushrooms

10½ oz (300 g) fatty ground pork

5 oz (150 g) raw large shrimp, peeled, deveined and coarsely chopped

3 tbsp (25 g) finely grated fresh ginger

1 tbsp (15 ml) light soy sauce

1 tbsp (15 ml) Shaoxing rice wine

1 tbsp (15 ml) sesame oil

½ tsp cornstarch

¼ tsp superfine sugar

¾ tsp salt

Pinch of freshly ground white pepper

35 Wonton Wrappers (page 141)

2 tbsp (25 g) finely chopped carrot

Roasted Sichuan Chile Oil (page 130), for serving

Make the filling: Soak the dried shiitake mushrooms in hot water until softened. Squeeze the excess water from the mushrooms, remove and discard the stems and chop finely. In a large bowl, combine the mushrooms with the remaining filling ingredients and mix vigorously in one direction until the mixture binds. Cover and let rest in the fridge for 1 hour.

To form a siu mai, make a circle with your thumb and index finger. Working with 1 wonton wrapper at a time, place 1 level teaspoon of filling in the center and nudge it down through the circle you've created with your hand. Gently squeeze it into shape and pat down the filling with the back of a spoon. Gently tap the dumpling on your work surface so it can stand upright, then top with a small pinch of carrot over the center. Repeat the process to form the remaining dumplings.

Line a bamboo steamer by placing your steamer basket on a sheet of parchment paper. Trace around the basket with a pencil and cut the paper with scissors. Place the cutout in the basket and carefully poke holes with a knife to allow for steam to come through. Place your basket in a wok. Pour enough water into the wok for the water line to reach 1 inch (2.5 cm) below the bottom of the steamer. Place the wok over high heat. Once the water is boiling, steam the siu mai in batches for 8 to 10 minutes, or until cooked through. Serve immediately with Roasted Sichuan Chile Oil.

NOTE

Superfine sugar can be replaced with granulated sugar when used in dumpling fillings. In sauces, dressings and where baking is required take extra care in ensuring the granulated sugar has dissolved properly.

CRYSTAL SHRIMP HAR GOW

Known as har gow in Cantonese, these plump and juicy shrimp dumplings are among the most popular items on offer as dim sum. They are packed full of flavor, visually enticing with a blush pink crystal appearance and perfect for entertaining. Although best eaten immediately from the steamer basket, har gow can be prepared well in advance, stored and enjoyed at a later date. You can tell a har gow is cooked when it has puffed slightly and the skin has become translucent.

MAKES 24 DUMPLINGS

Filling

12½ oz (350 g) raw large shrimp, peeled and deveined

Pinch of salt

1 tsp cornstarch

2 oz (56 g) bamboo shoots, finely chopped

2 oz (56 g) pork fat, minced (optional)

1 tsp finely grated fresh ginger

2 tsp (10 ml) oyster sauce

1 tsp sesame oil

1 tsp Shaoxing rice wine

½ tsp superfine sugar

Pinch of freshly ground white pepper

24 Crystal Dumpling Wrappers (page 141)

Make the filling: Soak the shrimp in cold water for 30 minutes to 1 hour. This will help maintain a firm texture after the cooking process. Remove the shrimp, pat dry and cut into coarse chunks. In a medium bowl, combine the shrimp with the salt and cornstarch and stir for 2 to 3 minutes in one direction with a pair of chopsticks. Add the remaining filling ingredients and continue to stir until sticky and well mixed. Cover and let rest in the fridge for 1 hour.

To assemble, place 1 level tablespoon (about 15 g) of filling in the center of a wrapper and shape into a crescent moon (see page 147). Repeat the process to form the remaining dumplings.

Line a bamboo steamer by placing your steamer basket on a sheet of parchment paper. Trace around the basket with a pencil and cut the paper with scissors. Place the cutout in the basket and carefully poke holes with a knife to allow for steam to come through. Place your basket in a wok. Pour enough water into the wok for the water line to be 1 inch (2.5 cm) below the bottom of the steamer. Place the har gow 1 inch (2.5 cm) apart in the steamer basket to allow for them to expand. Place the wok over high heat. Once the water is boiling, steam the har gow in batches for 6 to 8 minutes, or until the dumpling skin is transparent and the filling is firm and cooked through. Serve immediately.

NOTES

Canned bamboo shoots can be found at most Asian grocers. Immerse these in hot boiling water before chopping, to rid them of any unusual metallic flavor.

Obtain pork fat from pork fatback or cut it off a pork chop. Most butchers will be able to do this for you; otherwise, fatty bacon is a great substitute.

SWISS CHARD AND SPINACH JIAOZI

Jiaozi is a type of dumpling commonly eaten throughout most parts of China. As well as serving its purpose as a modest meal, it is considered a symbol of good fortune, resembling the shape of an ancient Chinese gold ingot, and is a must-have during Chinese Lunar New Year celebrations.

This specific recipe features a delicate vegetarian filling balanced out with the crunchy texture of water chestnuts and black fungus. The cooking method of steaming allows these dumplings to maintain their elegant shape and the subtle flavors inside.

MAKES 24 DUMPLINGS

Filling

Handful of dried black fungus

3 dried shiitake mushrooms

5 oz (150 g) Swiss chard leaves, stemmed and washed

5 oz (150 g) spinach, washed

5 oz (150 g) water chestnuts, finely chopped

5 tbsp (40 g) finely chopped fresh ginger

2 tbsp (30 ml) oyster sauce

2 tbsp (30 ml) sesame oil

Pinch of salt

24 Dumpling Wrappers (page 142)

Roasted Sichuan Chile Oil (page 130), for serving

Make the filling: Soak the dried black fungus and dried shiitake mushrooms separately in hot water until softened. Drain the black fungus well and chop finely. Squeeze the excess water from the mushrooms, remove and discard the stems and chop finely. Set aside.

Bring a large saucepan of water to a boil and blanch the Swiss chard and spinach for 30 seconds. Drain and refresh in cold water. Squeeze the excess water from the leaves and chop finely. In a large bowl, combine the black fungus, shiitake mushrooms, Swiss chard and spinach leaves with the remaining filling ingredients and mix well.

Working with 1 dumpling wrapper at a time, place 1 heaping tablespoon (20 g) of filling in the center of a wrapper and shape into a gold ingot half-moon (see page 149). Cover loosely with a clean, damp tea towel and repeat the process to form the remaining dumplings.

Line a bamboo steamer by placing your steamer basket on a sheet of parchment paper. Trace around the basket with a pencil and cut the paper with scissors. Place the cutout in the basket and carefully poke holes with a knife to allow for steam to come through. Place your basket in a wok. Pour enough water into the wok for the water line to be 1 inch (2.5 cm) below the bottom of the steamer. Place the wok over high heat. Once the water is boiling, steam the jiaozi in batches for 6 to 8 minutes, or until cooked through. Serve immediately with Roasted Sichuan Chile Oil.

NOTES

Dried black fungus can be found at most Asian grocers. It can be used interchangeably with fresh fungus or wood ear mushrooms, which are available at select supermarkets and health food stores.

Water chestnuts can be found canned at most Asian grocers. They can be replaced with canned lotus root.

SCALLOP AND GINGER DUMPLINGS

My rule of thumb when it comes to premium ingredients (particularly seafood) is to keep it simple, and this is what I have done here. These babies are delicate, buttery and bring out the natural sweetness of the scallops which, when paired with ginger, taste incredible.

Simple to make with only six ingredients, yet highly impressive at the table, these morsels are a must-try. Premake the filling and assemble the dumplings on the same day you are serving. With seafood, I believe it's best to always serve as fresh as possible. Oh, and don't forget to source the freshest scallops available. I kid you not: Regardless of your setting, guests will have a taste of these dumplings and believe they are sitting in a Michelin-starred restaurant.

MAKES 20 DUMPLINGS

Filling

10½ oz (300 g) fresh scallops, diced

3 green onions, finely sliced

3 tbsp (25 g) finely diced fresh ginger

2 tsp (10 ml) light soy sauce

1 tsp superfine sugar

1 tsp sesame oil

20 Wonton Wrappers (page 141)

Ginger-Soy Sticky Sauce (page 137), for serving

Roasted Sichuan Chile Oil (page 130), for serving

Julienned green onion, for garnish

Make the filling: In a medium bowl, combine all the filling ingredients and mix vigorously in one direction until the mixture binds. Cover and let rest in the fridge for 30 minutes.

Working with 1 wonton wrapper at a time, place 1 level tablespoon (15 g) of filling in the center. Dip your finger in water and moisten 2 adjoining edges of the wrapper. Gently lift the dry corner of the wrapper over the filling to meet the moist corner and lightly press around the filling to seal and create a triangle. Repeat this process to form the remaining dumplings.

Line a bamboo steamer by placing your steamer basket on a sheet of parchment paper. Trace around the basket with a pencil and cut the paper with scissors. Place the cutout in the basket and carefully poke holes with a knife to allow for steam to come through. Place your basket into a wok. Pour enough water into the wok for the water line to be 1 inch (2.5 cm) below the bottom of the steamer. Place the wok over high heat. Once the water is boiling, steam the dumplings in batches for 4 to 6 minutes, or until cooked through. Serve immediately with the Ginger-Soy Sticky Sauce, Roasted Sichuan Chile Oil and green onion.

PORK AND PEANUT DUMPLINGS

If you think that peanuts are a strange addition to a dumpling filling, I urge you to give this recipe a try. And if you, like me, are obsessed with peanuts, this dish has your name written all over it. Remember, the key to an exceptional pork and peanut dumpling is in the dry-roasting of the peanuts, so make sure you don't skip this step. The shiitake mushrooms also bring out an earthiness that complements the other flavors and savoriness of the pork. These are best when served immediately from the bamboo steamer. My favorite way to eat this dish is with a light and refreshing Smacked Cucumber Salad (page 111).

MAKES 30 DUMPLINGS

Filling

3 tbsp (27 g) unsalted peanuts

3 dried shiitake mushrooms

2 tbsp (30 ml) peanut oil

1 clove garlic, minced

Scant ¼ cup (30 g) finely grated ginger

8 oz (225 g) fatty ground pork

1 tbsp (8 g) cornstarch, mixed with 2 tbsp (30 ml) water

¼ cup (10 g) fresh cilantro, chopped

3 tbsp (18 g) sliced green onion

2 tbsp (30 ml) tamari

½ tsp superfine sugar

30 Crystal Dumpling Wrappers (page 141)

Make the filling: Preheat your oven to 350°F (180°C). Arrange the peanuts in a single layer on a dry baking sheet and bake, stirring at least once midway through, for 6 to 8 minutes, or until toasted and browned. Remove from the oven and allow to cool before chopping.

Soak the dried shiitake mushrooms in hot water until softened. Once soft, drain and squeeze the excess water from the mushrooms. Remove and discard the stems, chop finely and set aside.

Heat a medium skillet over medium heat and add the peanut oil. Add the garlic and ginger and cook, stirring, until fragrant, about 30 seconds. Add the pork and cook, stirring, until browned, about 5 minutes. Add the cornstarch slurry and stir, then continue to cook until thickened, about 30 seconds. Remove from the heat and mix in the shiitake mushrooms, cilantro, peanuts, green onion, tamari and sugar.

To assemble the dumplings, place 1 heaping teaspoon of filling in the center of a crystal dumpling wrapper and shape into a gold ingot (see page 149). Repeat the process to form the remaining dumplings.

Line a bamboo steamer by placing your steamer basket on a sheet of parchment paper. Trace around the basket with a pencil and cut the paper with scissors. Place the cutout in the basket and carefully poke holes with a knife to allow for steam to come through. Place your basket in a wok. Pour enough water into the wok for the water line to be 1 inch (2.5 cm) below the bottom of the steamer. Place the dumplings 1 inch (2.5 cm) apart in the steamer basket to allow for them to expand. Place the wok over high heat. Once the water is boiling, steam in batches for 6 to 8 minutes, or until the dumpling skin is transparent and the filling is firm and cooked through. Serve immediately.

SHANGHAI SOUP DUMPLINGS

Shanghai soup dumplings (*xiao long bao*) are a personal favorite of mine, but beware—they are dangerously delicious. Filled with piping hot, mouthwatering soup and a filling that is equally as tasty, they need to be approached with caution, as they can squirt if bitten into carelessly by the uninitiated. There is an art to eating these dumplings: First, dip your dumpling into the ginger vinegar sauce, then place it in your spoon. Poke a hole in the wrapper and slurp out all the juices. Eat!

There is no denying Shanghai soup dumplings are difficult to prepare, but start out with ones that are a little bigger than usual, then scale down as you gain confidence and skill. Avoid getting any filling on the edges and be sure to pinch firmly as you pleat, to create a tight seal.

MAKES 35 DUMPLINGS

- -

Ginger Vinegar Sauce

3 tbsp (45 ml) Chinese black vinegar

2 tsp (10 ml) tamari

2 tbsp (15 g) julienned fresh ginger

Pork Soup Jelly

4¼ oz (120 g) pork rind

6 tbsp (50 g) sliced fresh ginger

3 green onions, white part only

4 tsp (20 ml) Shaoxing rice wine

1½ cups (355 ml) water

Filling

2½ tbsp (20 g) finely grated fresh ginger

1 green onion, finely minced

½ cup (120 ml) just-boiled water

1 lb (450 g) fatty ground pork

4 tsp (20 ml) oyster sauce

2 tbsp + 2 tsp (40 ml) light soy sauce

2 tsp (12 g) salt

4 tsp (20 ml) sesame oil

1 tsp superfine sugar

35 Dumpling Wrappers (page 142)

Make the ginger vinegar sauce: In a small bowl, stir together all the sauce ingredients. Cover and refrigerate until needed.

Make the pork soup jelly: Fill a small saucepan with water and bring to a boil over high heat. Add the pork rind and cook for about 5 minutes, or until it becomes slightly translucent. Remove the pork rind and rinse the pan with water to remove any impurities. Cut the pork into small strips and place in a pressure cooker along with the ginger, green onions, Shaoxing rice wine and water. Cook on high pressure for 40 minutes. Let the soup cool down slightly, then use an immersion blender to process until smooth. Strain into an airtight container and refrigerate overnight.

Make the filling: Soak the ginger and green onion in the just-boiled water for 15 minutes. Place the pork in a large bowl and mix in one direction while slowly pouring in the ginger mixture until well combined. Mix in the remaining filling ingredients, cover and let rest in the fridge for 15 minutes. Remove the pork jelly from the fridge and mince with a knife. Mix into the filling.

To assemble, place 1 level tablespoon (about 15 g) of filling in the center of a wrapper and shape into a soup dumpling (see page 150). Repeat the process to form the remaining dumplings.

Line a bamboo steamer by placing your steamer basket on a sheet of parchment paper. Trace around the basket with a pencil and cut the paper with scissors. Place the cutout in the basket and carefully poke holes with a knife to allow for steam to come through. Place your basket in a wok. Pour enough water into the wok for the water line to be 1 inch (2.5 cm) below the bottom of the steamer. Place the Shanghai soup dumplings 1 inch (2.5 cm) apart in the steamer basket to allow for them to expand. Place the wok over high heat. Once the water is boiling, steam in batches for 6 to 8 minutes, or until the dumpling skin is transparent and the filling is firm and cooked through. Serve immediately with the ginger vinegar sauce for dipping.

NORTHERN-STYLE LAMB DUMPLINGS

You would be surprised at how popular lamb is in the northern and western parts of China. Similarly, it is also very popular at home within my family. The combination of cumin and lamb is a marriage made in heaven, and when done properly, is extremely addictive. A hint of Sichuan pepper adds to the bold flavors, along with a fiery and refreshing Sichuan Chile Dressing. Make this for your guests, and you will be sure to impress.

MAKES 30 DUMPLINGS

Filling

17½ oz (500 g) fatty ground lamb

1 tbsp (6 g) cumin seeds, toasted and ground

1 tsp Sichuan peppercorns, toasted and ground

7 tbsp (60 g) finely grated fresh ginger

2 green onions, finely sliced

2 tbsp (30 ml) light soy sauce

2 tbsp (30 ml) sesame oil

1 tbsp (15 ml) Shaoxing rice wine

1 large egg

Pinch of sea salt

½ tsp superfine sugar

30 Dumpling Wrappers (page 142)

Sichuan Chile Dressing (page 130), for serving

Chopped fresh cilantro, for garnish

Make the filling: In a large bowl, combine all the filling ingredients and mix vigorously in one direction until the mixture binds. Cover and let rest in the fridge for at least 30 minutes.

To assemble, place 1 level tablespoon (about 15 g) of filling in the center of a wrapper and shape into a gold ingot moon (see page 149). Repeat the process to form the remaining dumplings.

Line a bamboo steamer by placing your steamer basket on a sheet of parchment paper. Trace around the basket with a pencil and cut the paper with scissors. Place the cutout in the basket and carefully poke holes with a knife to allow for steam to come through. Place your basket in a wok. Pour enough water into the wok for the water line to be 1 inch (2.5 cm) below the bottom of the steamer. Place the lamb dumplings 1 inch (2.5 cm) apart in the steamer basket to allow for them to expand. Place the wok over high heat. Once the water is boiling, steam in batches for 6 to 8 minutes, or until the dumpling skin is transparent and the filling is firm and cooked through. Serve immediately with the Sichuan Chile Dressing and cilantro.

TOFU AND KIMCHI JIAOZI

The beauty of jiaozi is in its versatility. There are no strict rules when it comes to the filling, and although pork is the most common ingredient used, you can fill these delicious pouches with anything you desire. This recipe is a particularly special one for me, and one I created from scratch when developing our first vegan option for Bumplings—my pride and joy dumplings kitchen. The sweet, pungent spiciness added by the gochujang gives this dumpling its distinct flavor. Tofu not only helps bind the filling, it gives it a meatlike consistency. Oh, and if you like kimchi, then say no more—this one's for you!

MAKES 30 DUMPLINGS

- -

Filling

10½ oz (300 g) firm tofu

2 tbsp (30 ml) vegetable oil

½ red onion, finely diced

3 cloves garlic, minced

5 tbsp (40 g) finely grated fresh ginger

1 carrot, peeled and grated

1 cup (70 g) finely shredded napa cabbage

2 green onions, finely sliced

½ cup (75 g) kimchi, chopped

2 tbsp (30 ml) light soy sauce

1 tbsp (15 ml) sesame oil

1 tbsp (20 g) gochujang (Korean chili paste)

1 tsp salt

30 Dumpling Wrappers (page 142)

Make the filling: Drain the tofu and pat it dry with a paper towel. Stack three or four layers of paper towels on a plate and place the tofu on top. Stack another three or four layers of paper towels on the tofu, followed by another plate and a few heavy cans of food to help press the tofu down. Refrigerate for 30 minutes to press and dry.

In a large skillet, heat the vegetable oil over medium heat. Add the red onion and cook for 30 seconds, or until soft. Add the garlic and ginger and stir to combine, then cook for an additional 30 seconds. Add the carrot, cabbage and green onions and cook until the vegetables are soft and the cabbage is slightly translucent, about 2 minutes. Remove from the heat and transfer the vegetables to a bowl. Allow to cool.

Remove the tofu from the refrigerator and transfer to a large bowl. Using your hands, break the tofu into crumbs. Add the vegetables, kimchi, soy sauce, sesame oil, gochujang and salt, then stir until well combined.

Working with 1 dumpling wrapper at a time, place 1 heaping tablespoon (20 g) of filling in the center of a wrapper and shape into a half-moon (see page 146). Cover loosely with a clean, damp tea towel and repeat the process to form the remaining dumplings.

Line a bamboo steamer by placing your steamer basket on a sheet of parchment paper. Trace around the basket with a pencil and cut the paper with scissors. Place the cutout in the basket and carefully poke holes with a knife to allow for steam to come through. Place your basket in a wok. Pour enough water into the wok for the water line to be 1 inch (2.5 cm) below the bottom of the steamer. Place the dumplings 1 inch (2.5 cm) apart in the steamer basket to allow for them to expand. Place the wok over high heat. Once the water is boiling, steam in batches for 6 to 8 minutes. Serve immediately.

TWO

BOILED DUMPLINGS

You may have heard the term *shui jiao*, which translates to "water dumplings" in Chinese. As a matter of fact, this is the most popular method for cooking dumplings in Chinese households and mine, too. My childhood was formed on boiled dumplings, as was my obsession with Chinese food, and I have my Grandmère to thank for that.

If you would like to take up the challenge of making fresh dumplings for the first time, this chapter is a great starting point. I love the soft, pillowy texture and a cleaner finish that a boiled dumpling makes. The only downside with boiled dumplings is that sometimes they will not retain their original look. But that doesn't matter, right? They are only going to be eaten anyway. Rest assured, there's no fussing around with intricate shapes and folds in this chapter; it's just simple flavors and good honest food.

The fillings themselves are quite versatile, utilizing similar staple ingredients, and serve as a good introduction to creating a standard base dumpling filling using different proteins. At a glance, these recipes might seem similar with only some slight differences, but the notable variation comes out in the taste and flavor: from the sauces served with them and the broths that the dumplings are paired with to perfectly complement them.

Fried and steamed dumplings come with dipping sauces, but boiled dumplings come drenched in flavor! In brief, the dumplings get boiled first, so come out of the pot all wet and hot, and then before they're served up, they just get wetter and hotter as they're coated in sauce or dropped into soup before you eat them.

To make a boiled dumpling, it is best to use a flour that is higher in gluten. This in turn will result in a firmer dough and better finish once cooked. Roll the wrappers a little thicker to avoid the dumplings opening up throughout the cooking process.

SPICY SICHUAN PORK WONTONS

The Sichuan province boasts some of China's spiciest food—even for the real chile addicts. Amid the chile and spices, the hallmark Sichuan peppercorns make for a full sensory experience, with a numbing-tingling sensation that accompanies the fired-up palate.

These wontons have a very traditional Chinese dumpling filling with a silky-smooth wrapper. What makes this dish is all in the sauce—a Black Vinegar and Tamari dressing and homemade Roasted Sichuan Chile Oil. The "wonton fold" is one of the easier ones, so a good place to start for your first time. Salty, tangy, sweet, tingly and spicy—just go easy on the oil if you want it milder.

For the chile addicts: Sprinkle with extra red pepper flakes and toasted ground Sichuan peppercorns.

MAKES 35 WONTONS

Filling

10½ oz (300 g) ground pork

1 tbsp (6 g) finely chopped green onion, white part only

1 tsp finely grated fresh ginger

1 tbsp (15 ml) oyster sauce

1 tbsp (15 ml) soy sauce

1 tsp Shaoxing rice wine

½ tsp sesame oil

½ tsp superfine sugar

Pinch of ground white pepper

35 Wonton Wrappers (page 141)

Black Vinegar and Tamari (page 133), for serving

Sliced green onion, for garnish

Roasted Sichuan Chile Oil (page 130), for serving

Make the filling: In a medium bowl, combine the ground pork, green onion, ginger, oyster sauce, soy sauce, Shaoxing rice wine, sesame oil, sugar and white pepper. Mix vigorously in one direction until the mixture binds. Cover and let rest in the fridge for 30 minutes.

To assemble, place 1 wonton wrapper on a clean surface. Place 1 heaping teaspoon of the mixture in the center and shape using the classic wonton fold (see page 148). Cover loosely with a clean, damp tea towel and repeat the process to form the remaining dumplings.

Cook the wontons in a pot of boiling water until cooked through, 4 to 6 minutes. Remove from the water using a slotted spoon, and divide among serving bowls. Serve immediately with a generous amount of Black Vinegar and Tamari, sliced green onion and Roasted Sichuan Chile Oil.

CHICKEN AND GINGER JIAOZI

I daresay these are the best dumplings in the whole book. The stand-out flavor in this dish comes from the more fatty chicken cuts—so if you're into lean cuts of chicken, a heads-up, you're not going to like these dumplings. But there's method to my madness: Like adding more oil to any dish before serving, the additional oils released from the chicken fat while being cooked carry through the flavors of the marinade and the ginger to burst on your taste buds.

The meat should be chopped roughly to get a nice firm texture to bite into. Keep an eye out for young ginger, because old ginger can really pack a punch!

MAKES 24 DUMPLINGS

Filling

10½ oz (300 g) fatty ground chicken

5 tbsp (40 g) grated fresh ginger

2 tbsp + 2 tsp (40 ml) oyster sauce

4 tsp (20 ml) light soy sauce

2 tsp (10 ml) Shaoxing rice wine

2 tsp (10 ml) sesame oil

Pinch of ground white pepper

24 Dumpling Wrappers (page 142)

Black Vinegar and Tamari (page 133), for serving

Roasted Sichuan Chile Oil (page 130), for serving

Bang Bang Sauce (page 137), for serving

Julienned cucumber, for serving

Sliced green onion, for garnish (optional)

Chopped roasted peanuts, for garnish

Make the filling: In a medium bowl, combine all the filling ingredients and mix vigorously in one direction until the mixture binds. Cover and let rest in the fridge for 30 minutes.

Working with 1 dumpling wrapper at a time, place 1 level tablespoon (15 g) of filling in the center of a wrapper and shape into a half-moon (see page 146). Cover loosely with a clean, damp tea towel and repeat the process to form the remaining dumplings.

Cook the dumplings in a pot of boiling water until cooked through, 4 to 6 minutes. Remove from the water using a slotted spoon. Serve in bowls topped with Black Vinegar and Tamari, Roasted Sichuan Chile Oil, Bang Bang Sauce, cucumber, sliced green onion (if using) and roasted peanuts.

PORK AND GARLIC CHIVE JIAOZI

Garlic chives are exactly what they sound like—the more "garlicky" relative of standard chives—and can be used as a tastier substitute for standard chives (and even garlic, if you can't be bothered peeling garlic cloves). Garlic chives find their place in Chinese cooking in many egg-based favorites, doughs and broths, but feature prevalently in many dumplings—this recipe is no exception!

Garlic chives should be easily accessible from your run-of-the-mill Asian grocer, but don't fret too much if you can't find them—garlic and chives or green onions can be swapped in.

MAKES 35 DUMPLINGS

Filling

17½ oz (500 g) fatty ground pork

2½ tbsp (20 g) finely grated fresh ginger

¼ cup (12 g) finely chopped garlic chives

¼ cup (25 g) finely chopped green onion

Pinch of salt

Pinch of ground white pepper

1 tsp superfine sugar

2 tbsp (30 ml) light soy sauce

1 tbsp (15 ml) Shaoxing rice wine

1 tbsp (15 ml) sesame oil

35 Dumpling Wrappers (page 142)

Mum's Fried Garlic and Soy (page 134), for serving

Make the filling: In a medium bowl, combine all the filling ingredients and mix vigorously in one direction until the mixture binds. Cover and let rest in the fridge for 30 minutes.

Working with 1 dumpling wrapper at a time, place 1 level tablespoon (15 g) of filling in the center of a wrapper and shape into a half-moon (see page 146). Cover loosely with a clean, damp tea towel and repeat the process to form the remaining dumplings.

Cook the dumplings in a pot of boiling water until cooked through, 4 to 6 minutes. Remove from the water using a slotted spoon. Serve with Mum's Fried Garlic and Soy.

LOBSTER XO DUMPLINGS

XO Sauce coins its name from "extra old" cognac. In China, cognac itself is always in very high demand, whereas XO is in very large supply—the ubiquitous sauce featuring dried scallop (expensive) is thought of as a very luxurious sauce that finds its way onto just about any Chinese restaurant's menu.

Lobster always impresses—sweet, buttery meat with creamy, flaky flesh. Don't worry about over-cooking your expensive lobster—the wonton wrapper is going to keep all those delicious juices inside the dumpling.

MAKES 20 DUMPLINGS

Pickled Celery

2 long celery ribs, diced

1 cup (240 ml) pickling liquid (page 108)

Filling

7 oz (200 g) raw lobster meat, diced

7 oz (200 g) raw white fish, finely minced

2 oz (60 g) water chestnuts, finely chopped

1½ tsp (5 g) finely grated fresh ginger

4 tsp (5 g) minced fresh lemongrass

4 tsp (20 ml) tamari

4 tsp (20 ml) Shaoxing rice wine

1 tsp sesame oil

1 tsp superfine sugar

Pinch of salt

Pinch of ground white pepper

20 Dumpling Wrappers (page 142)

XO Sauce (page 138), for serving

Make the pickled celery: In a medium nonreactive bowl, combine the celery and pickling liquid. Cover and refrigerate for anywhere between 3 and 24 hours, or until needed.

Make the filling: In a separate medium bowl, combine all the filling ingredients and mix vigorously in one direction until the mixture binds. Cover and let rest in the fridge for 30 minutes.

Working with 1 dumpling wrapper at a time, place 1 heaping tablespoon (20 g) of filling in the center of a wrapper and shape into a half-moon (see page 146). Cover loosely with a clean, damp tea towel and repeat the process to form the remaining dumplings.

Cook the dumplings in a pot of boiling water until cooked through, 4 to 6 minutes. Remove from the water using a slotted spoon. Serve in bowls topped with XO Sauce and pickled celery.

KANG KUNG AND TOFU DUMPLINGS

These dumplings are my own twist on the stock standard spinach and tofu dumplings. *Kang kung* (morning glory, watercress or water spinach) is an incredibly delicious stir-fried green that any good Chinese restaurant can make (even if it's not on the menu—you can still order it!) and one I can't do without!

My love for watercress makes its way into these vegan dumplings, loaded with garlicky goodness and the peppery, sweet flavor of the watercress.

MAKES 24 DUMPLINGS

Filling

7 oz (200 g) firm tofu

7 oz (200 g) kang kung

2 green onions, thinly sliced

3½ tsp (10 g) finely grated fresh ginger

1 clove garlic, minced

4 tsp (20 ml) tamari

2 tsp (10 ml) Shaoxing rice wine

1 tsp sesame oil

2 tbsp (30 ml) vegetable oil

24 Dumpling Wrappers (page 142)

Roasted Sichuan Chile Oil (page 130), for serving

Chopped cilantro, for garnish

Make the filling: Drain the tofu and pat it dry with a paper towel. Stack three or four layers of paper towels on a plate and place the tofu on top. Stack another three or four layers of paper towels on the tofu, followed by another plate and a few heavy cans of food to help press the tofu down. Refrigerate for 30 minutes to press and dry before crumbling with your hands.

Place the kang kung on a heatproof plate and set the plate in a bamboo steamer basket. Place your basket in a wok. Pour enough water into the wok for the water line to be 1 inch (2.5 cm) below the bottom of the steamer. Place the wok over high heat. Once the water is boiling, steam the kang kung for about 5 minutes. Remove from the wok and let cool slightly. Squeeze the kang kung firmly with your hands to remove any excess water, then chop finely. Transfer to a medium bowl along with the tofu and the remaining filling ingredients. Stir until well combined.

Working with 1 dumpling wrapper at a time, place 1 level tablespoon (15 g) of filling in the center of a wrapper and shape into a gold ingot shape (see page 149). Cover loosely with a clean, damp tea towel and repeat the process to form the remaining dumplings.

Cook the dumplings in a pot of boiling water until cooked through, 4 to 6 minutes. Remove from the water using a slotted spoon, and serve with Roasted Sichuan Chile Oil and cilantro.

NOTE

Press the tofu (using the pressing technique) to remove all the excess moisture. If the tofu doesn't get dried out enough, the juices will start to seep out when boiling, leaving a soggy filling inside the dumpling. No thanks!

RED CURRY CHICKEN WONTON SOUP

This recipe is the result of a last-minute rush in the kitchen, making use of whatever I could find in the pantry and fridge at home to make a quick and easy dinner for my family. Thankfully, we always have leftover wontons stored in our freezer, so half of my job was done. I found some red curry paste, and voilà, my Red Curry Chicken Wonton Soup was born. I've refined this recipe slightly to include Thai basil and a perfectly balanced dumpling filling. Mum says it is one of the tastiest creations I've made to date.

SERVES 6

Filling

12½ oz (350 g) fatty ground chicken

1 small carrot, grated

2 green onions, finely chopped

1 tsp finely grated fresh ginger

2 tbsp (30 ml) soy sauce

½ tsp sesame oil

35 Wonton Wrappers (page 141)

Red Curry Soup

1 tbsp (15 ml) vegetable oil

1 onion, finely chopped

2 tbsp (15 g) finely grated fresh ginger

2 cloves garlic, minced

¼ cup (60 g) red curry paste

4 cups (946 ml) chicken stock

1 (13.5-oz [400-ml]) can coconut milk

2 tbsp (26 g) superfine sugar

1 tsp salt

1 bunch bok choy, trimmed

Fresh cilantro, for garnish

Sliced long red chiles, for garnish

Make the filling: In a medium bowl, combine all the filling ingredients and mix vigorously in one direction until the mixture binds. Cover and let rest in the fridge for 30 minutes.

To assemble, place 1 wonton wrapper on a clean surface. Place 1 heaping teaspoon of the mixture in the center and shape using the classic wonton fold (see page 148). Cover loosely with a clean, damp tea towel and repeat the process to form the remaining dumplings. Set aside until needed.

Make the red curry soup: In a large saucepan, heat the vegetable oil over medium heat. Add the onion, ginger and garlic and cook, stirring, for 1 minute, or until fragrant and soft. Add the red curry paste and cook for an additional minute. Whisk in the chicken stock, coconut milk, sugar and salt. Bring to a boil, then lower the heat and simmer for 10 minutes. Taste and season as desired.

To finish, add the wontons to the soup and cook for about 6 minutes. Add the bok choy and cook for an additional 2 minutes. To serve, divide the wontons and bok choy among six serving bowls. Ladle in some soup and top with cilantro and sliced chiles.

BEEF DUMPLINGS IN HOT AND SOUR SOUP

This Central Chinese dish showcases all the old faithful spices of Sichuan cuisine: Chinese five-spice powder, coriander, Sichuan peppercorns and chile! While dumplings are always a winner in my eyes, they are quite a simple component in this classic, meant to break up the complex soup they're in with a rich, savory flavor and textural contrast.

Most of the time consumed in making this dish comes from the hot and sour broth itself—save yourself some time by preparing the dumplings in advance and freezing them! But under no circumstances should time be cut from making and later enjoying this life-changing broth—the hot and sour soup is the main event. As the name suggests, the dish delivers.

SERVES 6

Filling

1 lb (450 g) fatty ground beef

3½ oz (100 g) finely chopped Chinese or regular celery

½ cup (75 g) fresh corn kernels

2 tbsp + 2 tsp (40 ml) light soy sauce

4 tsp (20 ml) Shaoxing rice wine

2 tsp (10 ml) sesame oil

1 tsp salt

1 tsp superfine sugar

½ tsp ground Sichuan peppercorns

30 Dumpling Wrappers (page 142)

¾ cup (180 ml) Spiced Vinegar Sauce (page 133), for serving

6 tbsp (90 ml) light soy sauce, for serving

2 tbsp (30 ml) sesame oil, for serving

Roasted Sichuan Chile Oil (page 130), for serving

3 green onions, chopped, for garnish

1 bunch cilantro, chopped, for garnish

Toasted sesame seeds, for garnish

Make the filling: In a medium bowl, combine all the filling ingredients and mix vigorously in one direction until the mixture binds. Cover and let rest in the fridge for 30 minutes.

Working with 1 dumpling wrapper at a time, place 1 heaping tablespoon (20 g) of filling in the center of a wrapper and shape into a half-moon (see page 146). Cover loosely with a clean, damp tea towel and repeat the process to form the remaining dumplings.

Cook the dumplings in a pot of boiling water until cooked through, 4 to 6 minutes. Remove from the water using a slotted spoon and reserve ¼ cup (60 ml) of the cooking water. Divide among six serving bowls. Add 2 tablespoons (30 ml) of Spiced Vinegar Sauce to each bowl, along with 1 tablespoon (15 ml) of light soy sauce, 1 teaspoon of sesame oil, the reserved cooking water and Roasted Sichuan Chile Oil to taste. Top with green onions, cilantro and toasted sesame seeds. Serve immediately.

CANTONESE-STYLE SHRIMP WONTON SOUP

My variation on this street vendor delight uses just shrimp in the wontons instead of the typical pork and shrimp combo. Living in coastal Western Australia, we're so privileged to have some of the best seafood on tap, so these shrimp-pure wontons are a reminder of just how lucky we are here on the west coast!

Although the broth might look similar to pho, it's only in the sense that it's clear and fresh. The appearance hides the unique richness it takes on from braising the pork bones and drawing out the flavorsome marrow within.

SERVES 4

- -

Pork Bone Broth

2 tbsp (30 ml) vegetable oil

2¼ lbs (1 kg) pork chuck bones

5 tbsp (40 g) sliced fresh ginger, divided

6 cups (1.4 L) cold water

1 tsp dried shrimp, rinsed

Salt

Filling

10½ oz (300 g) raw large shrimp, peeled, deveined and chopped

1 tbsp (3 g) coarsely chopped fresh cilantro

1 tbsp (6 g) thinly sliced green onion

1½ tsp (5 g) finely diced fresh ginger

1 tsp Shaoxing rice wine

1 tsp light soy sauce

¼ tsp superfine sugar

¼ tsp sesame oil

24 Wonton Wrappers (page 141)

7 oz (200 g) uncooked egg noodles (optional)

1 bunch bok choy, trimmed

Make the pork bone broth: In a large saucepan, heat the oil over high heat. Add the pork bones and half of the sliced ginger. Cook, stirring, for about 6 minutes, to brown. Add the water, remaining sliced ginger and dried shrimp. Bring to a boil, then lower the heat to low and skim away any impurities that rise to the surface. Cover and simmer for 3 to 4 hours, or until fragrant. Season with salt to taste.

Make the wonton filling: In a medium bowl, combine all the filling ingredients and mix vigorously in one direction until the mixture binds. Cover and let rest in the fridge for 30 minutes.

To assemble, place 1 wonton wrapper on a clean surface. Place 1 heaping teaspoon of the mixture in the center and shape using the classic wonton fold (see page 148). Cover loosely with a clean, damp tea towel and repeat the process to form the remaining dumplings.

Cook the wontons in a pot of boiling water until cooked through, 4 to 6 minutes. Remove from the water, using a slotted spoon, and divide among four serving bowls. If you are using the noodles, cook them in the boiling water for 3 to 5 minutes, or until cooked through, drain and divide among the serving bowls. Cook the bok choy in the boiling water until just cooked, about 2 minutes. Remove with a slotted spoon and divide among the serving bowls. Ladle the pork bone broth over the wontons, noodles and bok choy. Serve immediately.

THREE

FRIED DUMPLINGS

This chapter boasts some of my favorite dumplings ever.

Fried dumplings, like most fried things, are the most popular of the three cooking techniques for dumplings. A crispy finish often goes a long way.

It's undeniable how important flavor is; however, real food lovers don't eat purely for flavor, but for texture, too! Yet texture remains one of the most underappreciated and underrecognized elements of cooking. Fried dumplings overall can handle a much more robust filling than those cooked by other methods, and a firm, crispy crust is the perfect ode to the mouthwatering filling contained within.

To ensure you get the most delicious outcome, use a nonstick skillet for frying. Also, make sure to fold your dumpling into a shape with a flat surface at the bottom. This will provide a maximum surface area for crisping up and will help the dumpling stand upright. You may also boil dumplings in advance, toss them in oil and store them in the fridge to prevent sticking; you can then come back to these at a later point and panfry them to finish.

One of my favorite contemporary dumplings, the first recipe in this chapter, is an unconventional twist on an old-school dumpling. I was lucky enough to stumble across these precious babies in London at the Dumpling Shack, and I've been dreaming about them ever since. This dumpling doesn't just have a soft, savory filling on the inside and a crispy panfried crust; it has a soft steamed top, too! The ultimate dumpling.

While a touch more delicacy is required to get the most out of these dumplings as opposed to the boiled ones, even if some of your dumplings from the previous chapters don't look perfect with tight folds—deep-fry them! Everything tastes better deep-fried!

Grandmère's Fried Shrimp Wontons (page 56) are a family heirloom and legacy that we sell at my dumpling kitchen, Bumplings. Every week, these sell out because deep-fried dumplings are always people-pleasers! It's my pleasure to share this very special part of my life and family with everyone, too.

JUICY CHICKEN SHENG JIAN BAO

These are like the older sister dumpling to the xiao long bao (Shanghai Soup Dumpling [page 23]). Whereas the xiao long bao is very delicate and soft, the *sheng jian bao* is a bit more robust, with a tougher skin than her sister.

If you're relatively new to dumplings, this is a good recipe to work with as the wrapper is a little more forgiving than some of the finicky thin ones.

To me, this is the ultimate dumpling. It combines all the champions of Chinese cuisine with texture and juiciness—pretty much a panfried, juicy, steamy dumpling.

If you've got to try making just one dumpling from this book, make this the one!

MAKES 20 DUMPLINGS

Filling

1 cup (70 g) shredded napa cabbage

1 tsp salt

12½ oz (350 g) skinless, boneless chicken thighs, cubed

1 green onion, finely chopped

2 cloves garlic, minced

2 tsp (6 g) cornstarch

1 tsp Shaoxing rice wine

1 tsp sesame oil

1 tsp vegetable oil

Pinch of superfine sugar

Pinch of ground white pepper

Bao bun dough (page 86)

Vegetable oil, for frying

Chopped cilantro, for garnish

Make the filling: In a medium bowl, combine the napa cabbage and salt and massage with your hands. Set aside at room temperature for 15 minutes, or until softened. Using your hands, squeeze out any excess water from the cabbage and return the cabbage to the bowl.

In a food processor, process the cubed chicken until finely minced. Add the cabbage, green onion and garlic and pulse 3 or 4 times, or until incorporated. Transfer to a large bowl and mix in the remaining filling ingredients. Cover and refrigerate to marinate for at least 30 minutes.

Fill the dumplings: Shape the dough into a 1¼-inch (3-cm)-thick log and cut into 20 equal pieces. Roll each piece into a ball and allow to rest for 3 minutes. Flatten each dough ball with the palm of your hand and then, using a rolling pin, roll into a disk about 3⅛ inches (8 cm) in diameter. Place 1 heaping tablespoon (20 g) of filling in the center of a dough disk. Gather up the sides and enclose the filling, pinching to seal and flipping so the seam side is at the bottom. Continue the process with the remaining dough and filling.

Cook the dumplings: In a large nonstick skillet with a lid, heat 1 tablespoon (15 ml) of vegetable oil over medium-high heat. Working in batches, add the dumplings, seam side down. Press down firmly to flatten their base and cook, uncovered, until the base is golden brown, about 3 minutes. Add ½ cup (120 ml) of water to the pan and cover with the lid. Cook for 5 to 7 minutes. Remove the lid and continue to cook until the liquid has cooked off and the undersides of the dumplings are crisp again. If needed, add more oil to help crisp them up. Serve immediately with cilantro.

PANFRIED CHICKEN AND CABBAGE DUMPLINGS

This dumpling is one of the newest to my repertoire! I had a similar dumpling when dining one night at one of my favorite Chinese restaurants and was captivated by the sour, delicious and unmistakable tang of Chinese sauerkraut (*suan cai*) cut through it.

The original dumplings that inspired this dish used pork and some other Chinese staples, but I've decided to splice the same extra funk from the suan cai, with some of the winning components of my Chicken and Ginger Jiaozi (page 33). Tangy, tasty and too good not to try!

MAKES 24 DUMPLINGS

Filling

Vegetable oil, for frying

3½ tbsp (30 g) finely grated fresh ginger

3 tbsp (30 g) finely grated garlic

1½ cups (105 g) finely chopped napa cabbage

2 green onions, chopped

Pinch of salt

14 oz (400 g) fatty ground chicken

1 tsp sesame oil

2 tbsp (30 ml) light soy sauce

24 Dumpling Wrappers (page 142)

Vegetable oil, for frying

Mum's Fried Garlic and Soy (page 134), for serving

Make the filling: In a wok, heat 1 tablespoon (15 ml) of vegetable oil over medium heat. Add the ginger and garlic and cook, stirring constantly, for 30 seconds. Add the cabbage and cook for an additional 2 minutes. Add the green onions and salt and cook until the cabbage softens, about 2 minutes. Remove from the heat and let cool completely. Transfer to a large bowl and add the chicken, sesame oil and light soy sauce. Mix well to combine.

Working with 1 dumpling wrapper at a time, place 1 heaping tablespoon (20 g) of filling in the center of a wrapper and shape into a crescent moon (see page 147). Cover loosely with a clean, damp tea towel and repeat the process to form the remaining dumplings

Cook the dumplings: In a large nonstick skillet with a lid, heat 1 tablespoon (15 ml) of vegetable oil over medium-high heat. Working in batches, add the dumplings, pleated side up. Press down firmly to flatten their base and cook, uncovered, until the base is golden brown, about 3 minutes. Add ½ cup (120 ml) of water to the pan and cover with the lid. Cook for 5 to 7 minutes. Remove the lid and continue to cook until the liquid has cooked off and the undersides of the dumplings are crisp again. If needed, add more oil to help crisp them up. Serve the dumplings immediately with Mum's Fried Garlic and Soy.

PANFRIED PORK AND KIMCHI DUMPLINGS

In Korea, the standard dumplings filled with tangy spicy kimchi are known as mandu. I love Korean flavors, which is why I've tried to fuse some elements of both Chinese and Korean food into this book, and absolutely in these dumplings.

These dumplings are similar in concept to the Panfried Chicken and Cabbage Dumplings (page 51) that are infused with tart Chinese sauerkraut (suan cai), but have distinct flavor differences and are a twist on the conventional mandu. Kimchi has a more spicy, tangy and acidic flavor, whereas suan cai has no chile but an unmistakable sour bite.

Mandu, when fried, are often called *gun mandu*—you'll be gunning for these mandu!

MAKES 30 DUMPLINGS

Filling

3½ oz (100 g) firm tofu

5 oz (150 g) fatty ground pork

Scant ⅔ cup (100 g) kimchi, finely chopped

2 green onions, finely chopped

2 tbsp (15 g) finely grated fresh ginger

1 tsp sesame oil

1 large egg

1 tsp salt

30 Dumpling Wrappers (page 142)

Vegetable oil, for frying

Roasted Sichuan Chile Oil (page 130), for serving

Sliced cucumber, for garnish

Toasted sesame seeds, for garnish

Make the filling: Drain the tofu and pat it dry with a paper towel. Stack three or four layers of paper towels on a plate and place the tofu on top. Stack another three or four layers of paper towels onto the tofu, followed by another plate and a few heavy cans of food to help press the tofu down. Refrigerate for 30 minutes to dry.

Remove the tofu from the refrigerator and transfer to a large bowl. Using your hands, break the tofu into crumbs. Add the remaining filling ingredients and stir until well combined.

Working with 1 dumpling wrapper at a time, place 1 level tablespoon (15 g) of filling in the center of a wrapper and shape into a triangle (see page 144). Cover loosely with a clean, damp tea towel and repeat the process to form the remaining dumplings.

Cook the dumplings: In a large nonstick skillet with a lid, heat 1 tablespoon (15 ml) of vegetable oil over medium-high heat. Working in batches, add the dumplings, flat side down. Press down firmly to flatten their base and cook, uncovered, until the base is golden brown, about 3 minutes. Add ½ cup (120 ml) of water to the pan and cover with the lid. Cook for 5 to 7 minutes. Remove the lid and continue to cook until the liquid has cooked off and the undersides of the dumplings are crisp again. If needed, add more oil to help crisp them up. Serve the dumplings immediately with Roasted Sichuan Chili Oil, cucumber and sesame seeds.

CHINESE SPICY BEEF POTSTICKERS

Among many meats utilized in Chinese food, beef is one that really sings with some of the more fiery elements from Sichuan cuisine. The homemade roasted chile oil gives the beef some real firepower along with all the usual suspects: sesame oil, Shaoxing rice wine, white pepper, garlic and so on.

These dumplings are superspicy! But if you don't like them hot, halve the amount of chile oil that you add—the filling will still hold its texture. I love feeling the burn, but I also love to have a glass of soy milk on hand to quench it. Once the heat dissipates—round two!

This panfried dumpling recipe differs from most in this book, seeing as there's a golden crispy "skirt" gluing the dumplings together. I find a lot of satisfaction not only in the added textural element but in the crisp sound of breaking the dumplings apart before eating them!

MAKES 30 DUMPLINGS

Filling

1 lb (450 g) fatty ground beef

3½ oz (100 g) Chinese or regular celery, finely chopped

½ cup (75 g) fresh corn kernels

2 tbsp + 2 tsp (40 ml) light soy sauce

4 tsp (20 ml) Shaoxing rice wine

2 tsp (10 ml) sesame oil

1 tsp salt

1 tsp superfine sugar

½ tsp ground Sichuan peppercorns

30 Dumpling Wrappers (page 142)

Dumpling Skirt

3 tbsp (31 g) white rice flour

Scant 5 tbsp (70 ml) water, at room temperature

1½ cups + 3 tbsp (400 ml) boiling water

Vegetable oil, for frying

Roasted Sichuan Chile Oil (page 130), for serving

Chopped cilantro, for garnish

Make the filling: In a medium bowl, combine all the ingredients and mix vigorously in one direction until the mixture binds. Cover and let rest in the fridge for 30 minutes.

Working with 1 dumpling wrapper at a time, place 1 heaping tablespoon (20 g) of filling in the center of a wrapper and shape into a half-moon (see page 146). Cover loosely with a clean, damp tea towel and repeat the process to form the remaining dumplings.

Make the dumpling skirt: Place the rice flour in a medium bowl. While whisking, gradually add the room-temperature water. Whisk in the boiling water to make a milky slurry. Set aside, uncovered, until needed.

Cook the dumplings: In a large nonstick skillet with a lid, heat 1 tablespoon (15 ml) of vegetable oil over medium-high heat. Working in batches, add the dumplings, flat side down. Press down firmly to flatten their base and cook, uncovered, until the base is golden brown, about 3 minutes. Whisk the dumpling skirt mixture and pour about ½ cup (120 ml) of it into the pan. Cover with the lid and lower the heat to medium. Let simmer until most of the liquid has evaporated, 5 to 7 minutes. Remove the lid and continue to cook until the liquid has cooked off and a thin layer of skirt has formed. If needed, add more oil to help crisp them up. Shake gently if stuck and turn onto a serving plate. Serve immediately with Roasted Sichuan Chile Oil and cilantro.

GRANDMÈRE'S FRIED SHRIMP WONTONS

While I was growing up, Grandmère made her fried shrimp wontons a regular at any family gathering. Everyone loves deep-fried wontons!

In Australia, dumpling houses serve these with mayonnaise for dipping. You can have them like that, but my way calls for some chile and garlic dipping sauce (page 99) that pays homage to my Mauritian heritage—just how Grandmère used to make them. What really makes this recipe a winner is how easy these are to prepare, so it is probably a good one to start with, for its ease and also for being a classic Chinese dumpling. The wrapper and the fold itself don't need to look perfect—they're just going to get deep-fried anyway!

MAKES 24 WONTONS

Filling

10½ oz (300 g) raw large shrimp, peeled, deveined and diced

2 tbsp (30 ml) tamari

1 tbsp (3 g) finely chopped fresh cilantro leaves

1 tsp finely grated fresh ginger

1 green onion, finely sliced

1 tsp sesame oil

1 tsp Shaoxing rice wine

24 Wonton Wrappers (page 141)

Vegetable oil, for frying

Chile and garlic dipping sauce (page 99), for serving

Make the filling: In a medium bowl, combine all the filling ingredients and mix vigorously in one direction until the mixture binds. Cover and let rest in the fridge for 30 minutes.

Working with 1 dumpling wrapper at a time, place 1 heaping teaspoon of filling in the center of a wrapper and shape into a classic wonton fold (see page 148). Cover loosely with a clean, damp tea towel and repeat the process to form the remaining dumplings.

Cook the wontons: Fill a wok about two-thirds full with vegetable oil. Heat to 350°F (180°C) and test by dipping a wooden chopstick into the oil: The chopstick will sizzle when the oil is ready. Working in batches, gently lower the wontons into the oil and cook until golden brown, 3 to 5 minutes. Drain on a plate lined with paper towels and serve immediately with the chile and garlic dipping sauce.

NOTE

Make them an hour or so before serving—keep them hot in the oven on low heat.

FRIED BBQ PORK DUMPLINGS

If you're well versed in making dumpling wrappers, then this should be a pretty easy recipe to slap together. But if you don't have any Chinese BBQ pork (*char siu*) ready to go and don't have the time to put together their sticky, spicy and sweet marinade, there should be a Chinese restaurant in your neighborhood that prepares boneless spare ribs, a good substitute. Life hacks!

If you're well versed in Chinese food, you'll recognize the deep pink BBQ pork as a classic Chinese staple. This fried dumpling is a more modern fusion of this classic Chinese staple, with a hardier wrapper for a firm, crispy texture, instead of the heavy pastry as you might find in BBQ pork puffs at dim sum restaurants. For the puritans, a recipe for BBQ Pork Steamed Buns appears on page 91, but if you really love char siu—jump in here!

MAKES 35 DUMPLINGS

BBQ Pork Filling

1 tbsp (8 g) cornstarch

6 tbsp + 2 tsp (100 ml) water

1 tbsp (15 ml) vegetable oil

½ red onion, finely chopped

1 tbsp (15 ml) light soy sauce

1 tbsp (15 ml) oyster sauce

1 tbsp (15 ml) hoisin sauce

2 tsp (10 ml) sesame oil

1 tbsp (13 g) superfine sugar

2 cups (350 g) finely diced Chinese BBQ pork, store-bought

35 Dumpling Wrappers (page 142)

Vegetable oil, for frying

Roasted Sichuan Chile Oil (page 130), for serving

Make the filling: In a small bowl, whisk together the cornstarch with the water and set aside for 2 minutes.

In a wok, heat the vegetable oil over medium-high heat and add the red onion. Cook, stirring, for 1 minute. Lower the heat to medium-low and add the cornstarch slurry, light soy sauce, oyster sauce, hoisin sauce, sesame oil and sugar. Cook, stirring, until the mixture bubbles and thickens, about 3 minutes. Remove from the heat and stir in the diced BBQ pork. Let the filling cool slightly before covering and refrigerating for at least 30 minutes.

Working with 1 dumpling wrapper at a time, place 1 heaping teaspoon of filling in the center of a wrapper and shape into a simple potsticker shape (page 145). Cover loosely with a clean, damp tea towel and repeat the process to form the remaining dumplings.

Cook the dumplings: In a large nonstick skillet with a lid, heat 1 tablespoon (15 ml) of vegetable oil over medium-high heat. Working in batches, add the dumplings, seam side up. Press down firmly to flatten their base and cook, uncovered, until the base is golden brown, about 3 minutes. Add ½ cup (120 ml) of water to the pan and cover with the lid. Cook for 5 to 7 minutes. Remove the lid and continue to cook until the liquid has cooked off and the undersides of the dumplings are crisp again. If needed, add more oil to help crisp them up. Serve immediately with Roasted Sichuan Chile Oil.

NOTE

BBQ pork (char siu) can be found at most Chinese BBQ restaurants. You can also ask a staff member or one of the chefs if it's not on the menu.

CRISPY TARO DUMPLINGS

Taro is a relative of the sweet potato. Taro flesh is used in the dough for these dumpling wrappers, forming a subtly sweet and creamy layer around a classic pork filling. Although taro itself can be quite starchy and heavy, the baking soda in the dough makes the outside layer superairy and light.

MAKES 12 DUMPLINGS

Filling

3½ oz (100 g) fatty ground pork

2 tsp (10 ml) light soy sauce

Scant 4 tsp (10 g) finely grated fresh ginger

Pinch of salt

Pinch of ground white pepper

Pinch of superfine sugar

1 tsp cornstarch

Dash of sesame oil

2 tsp (10 ml) oyster sauce

1 tsp Shaoxing rice wine

4 tsp (20 ml) water

4 tsp (20 ml) vegetable oil

2 green onions, chopped

Crispy Taro Dough

14 oz (400 g) taro root

⅓ cup (43 g) wheat starch

⅓ cup (80 ml) boiling water

Pinch of salt

1 tsp superfine sugar

Scant 5 tbsp (63 g) lard or 5 tbsp (70 g) unsalted butter, at room temperature

Vegetable oil, for frying

Make the filling: In a small bowl, combine the pork, soy sauce and ginger and stir well. Heat a small skillet over medium heat, add the pork mixture and cook, stirring constantly to break into smaller pieces, until cooked through, 5 to 7 minutes. Remove from the heat and transfer to a medium bowl. Mix in the remaining filling ingredients. Cover and refrigerate for at least 4 hours.

Make the dough: Peel the taro root and chop into 1-inch (2.5-cm) chunks. Steam the taro chunks over boiling water for about 45 minutes, or until soft. Place the wheat starch in a medium heatproof bowl and, while stirring with a wooden spoon, gradually add the boiling water. When the mixture resembles cake frosting, cover with plastic wrap and set aside.

Remove the taro from the steamer and let it cool slightly. Transfer to a bowl and mash with your hands, removing any hard pieces. Place 1 cup (225 g) of the mashed taro in the bowl along with the wheat starch mixture and add the salt and sugar. Use your hands to mix and slowly work in the lard. Knead until the texture resembles that of mashed potatoes, then form into a ball and wrap in plastic wrap. Refrigerate for at least 2 hours.

Assemble the dumplings: Line a baking sheet with parchment paper. Place the dough on a work surface and shape into a log, cut into 12 equal pieces and roll each piece into a ball. Allow to rest, refrigerated, for 10 minutes. Working with one ball of dough at a time (keep the remaining balls of dough in the refrigerator), flatten into an oval shape and fill with a teaspoon of filling. Bring the edges together and pinch to make a football shape. Patch any holes with extra dough and place on the prepared pan. Continue the process with the remaining dough and filling.

Cook the dumplings: Fill a wok about two-thirds full with vegetable oil. Heat to 350°F (180°C) and test by dipping a wooden chopstick into the oil: The chopstick will sizzle when the oil is ready. Working in batches of about 4 at a time, gently lower the dumplings into the oil and cook until golden brown, 3 to 5 minutes. Drain on a plate lined with paper towels and serve immediately.

FOUR

RAINBOW DUMPLINGS

The beauty of dumplings is that once you have mastered some of the basic skills, you have license to play around and be creative. Don't be bound by the recipes if you've got a good grip on the techniques; have some fun and express your colorful side, too—that's exactly what I did with these!

Taste is at the foundation of why we eat, but food can be so much more than that! Appearance plays such a significant role when it comes to food. I truly believe you eat with your eyes, and for me the enjoyment starts when something that looks delicious catches your eye—before it's even hit your palate. But it's not just about aesthetic value. Did you know that the bright colors that naturally occur in many fruits and vegetables come from natural pigments or colorings that also have profound nutritional value?

To name a few: Purple beets contain betalains; the blue pigment in some foods comes from anthocyanins; dark green, leafy vegetables are rich in chlorophyll; yellow turmeric contains curcumin; beta-carotene is prevalent in many orange foods; and the bright red hue of tomatoes comes from lycopene. Some of these foods are called "functional foods," because their vibrant colors come with health benefits!

These pigments are rich in all the good things that help to keep us healthy, have antioxidant and anti-inflammatory actions and best of all, are naturally occurring!

Not only is my ethos to "eat with your eyes," but I also believe in "eating a rainbow" of good foods. These are the main focuses I've tried to incorporate into this colorful chapter, in addition to showcasing a diverse range of tastes and flavors that symbolize the color and theme of each recipe.

The take-home message: The brighter and more colorful these natural foods are, the better it is for you. I swear by natural-colored dyes (which you can make at home), and no one loves playing with colors more than kids! What I know is my little brothers love making rainbow dumplings, so this is a great chapter for bringing the family together and getting the kids cooking in the kitchen, too!

GREEN: CHICKEN AND CILANTRO DUMPLINGS

This dumpling begins the rainbow journey. It is an easy recipe with just six ingredients for the filling and is everything you want in a dumpling—tasty, juicy and fresh. Like many of the recipes in this chapter, these dumplings really shine as potstickers, whereby they get a little crispy panfried bottom, but retain the streamed firm top. These dumplings get their lush, verdant green wrapper from a spinach puree—such a great, innocuous way to get your daily serving of greens (especially for young kids who don't eat all their greens, as I used not to!).

MAKES 30 DUMPLINGS

- -

Colored Wrappers

1⅓ cups (40 g) spinach leaves

6 tbsp + 2 tsp (100 ml) water, plus more if needed

30 green Rainbow Dumpling Wrappers (page 142)

Filling

1 lb (450 g) boneless, skinless chicken thighs, cut into ⅜-inch (1-cm) cubes

1 bunch cilantro, roughly chopped

4 cloves garlic, halved

6 tbsp (50 g) chopped fresh ginger

3 tbsp + 1 tsp (50 ml) soy sauce

1 tbsp (15 ml) sesame oil

Fragrant Cilantro Oil

1 large bunch cilantro, roots removed

1 cup (240 ml) grapeseed oil

⅓ cup (45 g) ginger, skin on, thinly sliced

Vegetable oil, for frying

Make the wrappers: Combine the spinach and water in a blender and blend until smooth. Add another tablespoon (15 ml) of water at a time if gluggy and blend for an additional 20 seconds. Strain and use to make the green rainbow dumpling wrappers.

Make the filling: In a food processor, combine all the filling ingredients and process on low speed for about 30 seconds, or until finely chopped. Cover and refrigerate for about 30 minutes.

Prepare the cilantro oil by placing a small pot of water over high heat. Once boiling, turn the heat off and plunge the cilantro into the hot water. Remove and plunge immediately into an iced water bath to refresh and stop the cooking process. Squeeze it firmly with your hands to remove all liquid and set aside until required. Place the grapeseed oil and ginger in a small pot over medium heat. Once the ginger is sizzling, turn the heat to low and let cook for a further 15 minutes. Remove from the heat and let cool completely to room temperature. Strain the oil into a blender and add the blanched cilantro. Blend on high speed until the oil is vibrant green in color. Strain through a sieve lined with muslin cloth into a bowl and set aside.

Working with 1 dumpling wrapper at a time, place 1 level tablespoon (15 g) of filling in the center of a wrapper and shape into a half-moon shape (see page 146). Cover loosely with a clean, damp tea towel and repeat the process to form the remaining dumplings.

Cook the dumplings: In a large nonstick skillet with a lid, heat 1 tablespoon (15 ml) of vegetable oil over medium-high heat. Working in batches, add the dumplings, pleated side up. Press down firmly to flatten their base and cook, uncovered, until the base is golden brown, about 3 minutes. Add ½ cup (120 ml) of water to the pan and cover with the lid. Cook for 5 minutes. Remove the lid and continue to cook until the liquid has cooked off and the undersides of the dumplings are crisp again. If needed, add more oil to help crisp them up.

RED: KOREAN BEEF DUMPLINGS

I was first properly introduced to Korean food and flavors only a year ago. I was lucky enough to work with two Korean chefs who showed me some traditional Korean dishes, such as *gamjatang* and *tteokbokki*—these are the kind of things on a menu that you wouldn't know to order unless you've got someone leading you. I was also lucky enough to learn a true Korean favorite, which also happens to be a dumpling: the mandu!

Many times in this book I talk about the heat of Sichuan food from central China, and when I think of the color red, I think of heat, fire and spice. While this is based on a very authentic Korean mandu, most Korean food isn't punishingly spicy, so this recipe is definitely Sichuan-inspired in that it brings the fire. My twist accentuates the umami-ness of the kimchi with beef, and really kicks the heat up a notch for the true embodiment of the color red. You'll need to channel your inner artist for these dumplings—you've got to mix some colors up! The combination of the deep purple hue from beets and the intensely yellow turmeric gives a powerful Chinese red.

MAKES 40 DUMPLINGS

Colored Wrappers

6 tbsp + 2 tsp (100 ml) water

¾ oz (20 g) beet chunks

¼ oz (5 g) fresh turmeric

40 red Rainbow Dumpling Wrappers (page 142)

Filling

7 oz (200 g) firm tofu

8 oz (225 g) uncooked sweet potato starch noodles

¾ cup (112 g) kimchi, plus extra for garnish

10½ oz (300 g) mung bean sprouts

3 green onions, finely chopped

7 oz (200 g) fatty ground beef

1½ tbsp (15 g) finely minced garlic

2 tsp (5 g) finely grated fresh ginger

1 tbsp (15 ml) sesame oil

1 tbsp (15 ml) soy sauce

1 tbsp (6 g) gochugaru (Korean chili flakes)

Salt

Ground white pepper

Make the colored wrappers: In a blender, combine the water, beet and turmeric and blend until smooth. Add another tablespoon (15 ml) of water at a time if gluggy and blend for an additional 20 seconds. Strain and use to make the red rainbow dumpling wrappers.

Make the filling: Drain the tofu and pat dry with a paper towel. Stack three or four layers of paper towels on a plate and place the tofu on top. Stack another three or four layers of paper towels onto the tofu, followed by another plate and a few heavy cans of food to help press the tofu down. Refrigerate for 30 minutes to press and dry.

Soak the noodles in warm water for 30 minutes, then drain and chop finely. Squeeze any excess liquid from the kimchi by hand and finely chop. Blanch the bean sprouts in boiling water, drain, chop and squeeze out the water.

Remove the tofu from the refrigerator and transfer to a large bowl. Using your hands, break the tofu into crumbs. Add the noodles, kimchi, bean sprouts and the remaining filling ingredients, including a pinch each of salt and ground white pepper, and stir until well combined.

(continued)

RED: KOREAN BEEF DUMPLINGS (CONT.)

Vegetable oil, for frying

Kimchi, for serving

Working with 1 dumpling wrapper at a time, place 1 heaping tablespoon (20 g) of filling in the center of a wrapper and shape into a gold ingot shape (see page 149). Cover loosely with a clean, damp tea towel and repeat the process to form the remaining dumplings.

Cook the dumplings: In a large nonstick skillet with a lid, heat 1 tablespoon (15 ml) of vegetable oil over medium-high heat. Working in batches, add the dumplings, pleated side up. Press down firmly to flatten their base and cook, uncovered, until the base is golden brown, about 3 minutes. Add ½ cup (120 ml) of water to the pan and cover with the lid. Cook for 5 to 7 minutes. Remove the lid and continue to cook until the liquid has cooked off and the undersides of the dumplings are crisp again. If needed, add more oil to help crisp them up. Serve with a side of kimchi.

PINK: CHINESE ROAST DUCK DUMPLINGS

Duck is only mentioned in one other place in this book, but it is one of best and most special meats, in my opinion! This started early on in life for me when we'd have a lazy family meal, entailing a spread of various roast meats from the Chinese BBQ shop—but I'd only have eyes (and the stomach) for the duck!

Not only is it a major player in Chinese food, but roast duck also finds its home alongside sweet sauces, such as plum sauce. Sweet sauces can be too heavy when paired with the richness of duck, so I've drawn on a wine pairing for some inspiration—pinot noir. Light, aromatic and dry, pinot noir cuts through the fatty richness of duck, with some fresh cranberries added for a tart edge and a bit of sticky sweetness. I believe this combo in the sauce balances out these duck dumplings beautifully.

Beet is used here for its beautiful pink tones. Make separate batches of pink wrappers using different amounts of beet puree in each batch of dough to create a range of the color's intensity—arranging a wave of dumplings in all different shades of pink is absolutely mesmerizing. Serve with a glass of pinot noir!

MAKES 30 DUMPLINGS

Colored Wrappers

6 tbsp + 2 tsp (100 ml) water

¾ oz (20 g) beet

30 pink Rainbow Dumpling Wrappers (page 142)

Cranberry and Pinot Noir Sauce

1 tbsp (15 ml) vegetable oil, for cooking

1 cup (100 g) fresh or frozen cranberries

2 tbsp (15 g) finely grated fresh ginger

1 cup + 2 tsp (250 ml) pinot noir

¾ cup (150 g) superfine sugar

½ tsp curry powder

Pinch of Chinese five-spice powder

Pinch of salt

Pinch of ground white pepper

Make the colored wrappers: In a blender, combine the water and beet and blend until smooth. Add another tablespoon (15 ml) of water at a time if gluggy and blend for an additional 20 seconds. Strain and use to make the pink rainbow dumpling wrappers.

Make the cranberry and pinot noir sauce: In a large saucepan, heat the vegetable oil over medium heat. Add the cranberries and ginger and stir until the cranberries start to burst and soften, 3 to 5 minutes. Add the pinot noir and sugar, then boil until the mixture is reduced to about 1 cup (240 ml), about 10 minutes. Add the curry powder, Chinese five-spice powder, salt and white pepper and mix well. Remove from the heat and set aside until needed.

(continued)

PINK: CHINESE ROAST DUCK DUMPLINGS (CONT.)

Filling

17½ oz (500 g) Chinese roast duck, shredded, store-bought

3 green onions, finely chopped

1 clove garlic, finely minced

2 tbsp (15 g) finely grated fresh ginger

1 tsp Chinese five-spice powder

5 tsp (25 ml) hoisin sauce

Pinch of salt

Pinch of ground white pepper

Vegetable oil, for frying

Make the filling: In a medium bowl, combine all the filling ingredients and stir until well combined.

Working with 1 dumpling wrapper at a time, place 1 level tablespoon (15 g) of filling in the center of a wrapper and shape into a simple potsticker (see page 145). Cover loosely with a clean, damp tea towel and repeat the process to form the remaining dumplings.

Cook the dumplings: In a large nonstick skillet with a lid, heat 1 tablespoon (15 ml) of vegetable oil over medium-high heat. Working in batches, add the dumplings, pleated side up. Press down firmly to flatten their base and cook, uncovered, until the base is golden brown, about 3 minutes. Add ½ cup (120 ml) water to the pan and cover with the lid. Cook for 5 to 7 minutes. Remove the lid and continue to cook until the liquid has cooked off and the undersides of the dumplings are crisp again. If needed, add more oil to help crisp them up. Serve with the cranberry and pinot noir sauce on the side for dipping or drizzled on top.

NOTE

Roast duck can be found at most Chinese BBQ and specialty roast duck restaurants. You can also ask a staff member or one of the chefs if it's not on the menu.

ORANGE: PORK, CARROT AND GINGER BAOZI

In a recent collaboration with Chinatown London, I got the opportunity to perfect these dumplings while working with the restaurant Dumpling Legend under the incredibly talented dumpling chef Xian Bing. The objective for me was to make a unique dumpling with very familiar and approachable dim sum flavors, but with my own artistic flair. I'm proud to say this opportunity and dumpling were a total success, and this recipe is nothing but proof of that!

One important thing that I really like about this recipe—they're big boys! A big portion size means a good eating, and freeze what you can't eat for future use. These buns are a must-have with a wrapper that is colored with carrot juice and a filling that carries this flavor within! Not only does carrot yield a vivid orange pigment (which comes from the potent antioxidant beta-carotene), but it also carries a delicate natural sweetness that truly blossoms in these baozi.

MAKES 15 BUNS

Colored Wrappers

6 tbsp + 2 tsp (100 ml) water

2 oz (60 g) carrot

¼ oz (5 g) fresh turmeric

15 orange Rainbow Dumpling Wrappers (page 142)

Filling

9 oz (250 g) fatty ground pork

1 tsp sesame oil

1 tbsp (15 ml) light soy sauce

5 tbsp (75 ml) vegetable oil, divided

Pinch of ground white pepper

1 tsp salt

3 large carrots, finely grated

3 green onions, finely chopped

2½ tbsp (20 g) finely grated fresh ginger

1 tsp Shaoxing rice wine

Vegetable oil, for frying

Toasted sesame seeds, for garnish

Roasted Sichuan Chile Oil (page 130), for serving

Chopped green onion, for garnish

Chopped cilantro, for garnish

To make the colored wrappers: In a blender, combine the water, carrot and turmeric and blend until smooth. Add another tablespoon (15 ml) of water at a time if gluggy and blend for an additional 20 seconds. Strain and use to make the orange rainbow dumpling wrappers.

Make the filling: In a medium bowl, combine the pork, sesame oil, soy sauce, 3 tablespoons (45 ml) of the vegetable oil, white pepper and salt and stir until well mixed. In a small skillet, heat the remaining 2 tablespoons (30 ml) of vegetable oil over medium heat and sauté the grated carrot until just cooked, 3 to 5 minutes. Remove from the heat and let cool. Once cool, add the cooked carrot to the pork mixture along with the remaining filling ingredients and mix vigorously in one direction until the mixture binds. Cover and let rest in the fridge for 30 minutes.

Working with 1 dumpling wrapper at a time, place 1 heaping tablespoon (20 g) of filling in the center of a wrapper and shape into a soup dumpling shape (see page 150). Cover loosely with a clean, damp tea towel and repeat the process to form the remaining dumplings.

Cook the buns: Place the buns in a large, deep, lidded skillet in a single layer. Pour in about 1 tablespoon (15 ml) of oil and water, or pour in a little oil and water, up to a third of the way up the buns. Cover and cook over medium-high heat until the water evaporates and the bottom of the buns are golden brown, 8 to 10 minutes. Remove the buns from the pan and sprinkle with sesame seeds. Serve immediately with Roasted Sichuan Chile Oil, green onion and cilantro.

YELLOW: CURRIED BEEF DUMPLINGS

When I think of yellow, I think of gold, and one of my guilty pleasures is golden curry. This is a very standard Japanese-style curry that has some pretty approachable flavors and heat levels for those averse to curry.

Golden curry has some base Indian spices, including fenugreek, cumin, coriander and turmeric, but a sweeter backbone that combines well with a savory and hearty type of meat. And that's exactly what I've done in this recipe—taken some delicious fatty beef, matched it with the tempered "curry" elements of golden curry and left these flavors to marinate and intensify for a more off-base dumpling filling. Make the filling in advance and let marinate for at least an hour for maximum flavor. A little different from your average dumpling filling, but honestly, this will blow your mind. I know, big call right?

You could go to all the effort to make golden curry from scratch, but honestly, I am not ashamed to admit that my preference is S&B brand Golden Curry Sauce mix. Not kidding. It's so wrong, but so right.

MAKES 15 DUMPLINGS

Colored Wrappers

6 tbsp + 2 tsp (100 ml) water

1 oz (30 g) fresh turmeric

15 yellow Rainbow Dumpling Wrappers (page 142)

Filling

2½ tbsp (20 g) chopped fresh ginger

2 green onions, white part only, chopped

½ tsp Sichuan peppercorns

⅓ cup (80 ml) boiling water

9 oz (250 g) fatty ground beef

Pinch of salt

Pinch of ground white pepper

3 tbsp + 1 tsp (50 g) golden curry paste

1 large egg

1 tbsp (15 ml) sesame oil

Vegetable oil, for frying

Cucumber

Black Vinegar and Tamari (page 133)

Make the colored wrappers: In a blender, combine the water and turmeric and blend until smooth. Strain and use to make the yellow rainbow dumpling wrappers.

Make the filling: In a small heatproof bowl, combine the ginger, green onions, Sichuan peppercorns and boiling water. Stir well and set aside to cool down to room temperature, about 15 minutes.

In a separate medium bowl, combine the beef, salt, white pepper, golden curry paste, egg and sesame oil. Strain the liquid from the ginger mixture into the bowl and mix vigorously in one direction until well combined. Cover and refrigerate for about 60 minutes.

Working with 1 dumpling wrapper at a time, place 1 heaping tablespoon (20 g) of filling in the center of a wrapper and shape into a simple potsticker shape (see page 145). Cover loosely with a clean, damp tea towel and repeat the process to form the remaining dumplings.

Cook the dumplings: In a large nonstick skillet with a lid, heat 1 tablespoon (15 ml) of vegetable oil over medium-high heat. Working in batches, add the dumplings, pleated side up. Press down firmly to flatten their base and cook, uncovered, until the base is golden brown, about 3 minutes. Add ½ cup (120 ml) of water to the pan and cover with the lid. Cook for 5 to 7 minutes. Remove the lid and continue to cook until the liquid has cooked off and the undersides of the dumplings are crisp again. If needed, add more oil to help crisp them up. Just before serving, thinly shave a cucumber lengthwise and toss it with a little Black Vinegar and Tamari. Serve immediately with the dumplings.

BLUE: CHILE MUD CRAB DUMPLINGS

Crab is one of my favorite seafoods, and always takes me back to some of the best times I spent up in the coastal north of Western Australia, where I'd spend my weekends hunting crabs. I was lucky enough to immerse myself in the indigenous culture of the warm and welcoming Yawuru people up there, where crabbing is a regular activity for the community. This blue dumpling is my way to appreciate water, and pays homage to the special times I had with the Yawuru people. For similar reasons, the base of the filling is mud crab, with a whip of chile and an Australian native plant called samphire, used by the Australian indigenous people.

MAKES 24 DUMPLINGS

Colored Wrappers

6 tbsp + 2 tsp (100 ml) water

1 tsp blue spirulina

24 blue Rainbow Dumpling Wrappers (page142)

Filling

4 tsp (20 ml) vegetable oil

½ onion, chopped

1 tbsp (10 g) minced garlic

4 tsp (10 g) finely grated fresh ginger

1½ tsp (2 g) red pepper flakes

1⅔ cups (150 g) chopped cabbage

1½ tsp (4 g) cornstarch

1 tbsp (15 ml) sweet soy sauce

3 tbsp (45 ml) tomato sauce

½ tsp fresh lemon juice

7 oz (200 g) mud crab meat

1 green onion, finely sliced

1 tbsp (3 g) chopped fresh cilantro

2 tbsp (4 g) samphire (see note)

Pinch of salt

Vegetable oil, for frying

Roasted Sichuan Chile Oil (page 130), for serving

Black Vinegar and Tamari (page 133), for serving

Make the colored wrappers: In a blender, combine the water and blue spirulina and blend until smooth. Use to make blue rainbow dumpling wrappers.

Make the filling: In a large nonstick skillet, heat the oil over medium heat. Add the onion, garlic and ginger and sauté until the onion softens and becomes translucent, 3 to 5 minutes. Add the red pepper flakes and cook for an additional minute. Add the cabbage, cornstarch and sweet soy sauce and cook until the cabbage softens, 5 to 7 minutes. Add the tomato sauce and lemon juice and cook, stirring, until the sauce has thickened, about 3 minutes. Add the crabmeat, green onion, cilantro, samphire and salt and stir to incorporate. Remove from the heat and let cool.

Working with 1 dumpling wrapper at a time, place 1 heaping tablespoon (20 g) of filling in the center of a wrapper and shape into a crescent moon shape (see page 147). Cover loosely with a clean, damp tea towel and repeat the process to form the remaining dumplings.

Cook the dumplings: In a large nonstick skillet with a lid, heat 1 tablespoon (15 ml) of vegetable oil over medium-high heat. Working in batches, add the dumplings, pleated side up. Press down firmly to flatten their base and cook, uncovered, until the base is golden brown, about 3 minutes. Add ½ cup (120 ml) of water to the pan and cover with the lid. Cook for 5 to 7 minutes. Remove the lid and continue to cook until the liquid has cooked off and the undersides of the dumplings are crisp again. If needed, add more oil to help crisp them up. Serve with Roasted Sichuan Chile Oil and Black Vinegar and Tamari.

NOTE

Samphire has a beautiful natural saltiness. It might not be readily accessible to you, so replace it with any green leafy vegetable, ideally watercress, and salt it well!

PURPLE: MISO ROASTED EGGPLANT POTSTICKERS

Purple produce are generally considered to be superfoods because, among the vitamin and mineral richness that they have, the deep purple tones they get from the pigment anthocyanin are thought to have profound antiaging effects! Yet not a lot of people eat purple—time to start? The purple is inescapable in this dumpling, as the wrapper uses purple cabbage for its royal purple hue, and inside, purple eggplant forms the base of the filling.

Eggplant is a vegetable that is terrible if not done properly, but that is not an option for this recipe! Even after cooking, eggplant holds its texture, so this gives the impression of meatiness upon biting into this dumpling. Salty, savory miso is one of the usual suspects in Japanese cuisine. In these dumplings, it really gets taken to the next level upon its caramelization, where nutty, sweet flavors emerge that balance out the umami backbone and draw out the natural sweetness of the eggplant it coats.

This dumpling's theme is all about expressing the natural goodness of going vegan, and that you don't need meat to have a tasty dumpling!

MAKES 30 DUMPLINGS

Colored Wrappers

6 tbsp + 2 tsp (100 ml) water

2 oz (60 g) purple cabbage

30 purple Rainbow Dumpling Wrappers (page 142)

Filling

1 large eggplant, about 1½ lbs (680 g)

4 tsp (20 g) white miso paste

2 tsp (10 ml) honey

3 tbsp (45 ml) tamari

1 tbsp (15 ml) white vinegar

1 tbsp (15 ml) ginger syrup

1 tbsp (15 ml) toasted sesame oil

2 tbsp (16 g) sesame seeds

Vegetable oil, for frying

Black Vinegar and Tamari (page 133), for serving

Finely sliced fresh chives, for garnish

Make the colored wrappers: In a blender, combine the water and purple cabbage and blend until smooth. Add another tablespoon (15 ml) of water if gluggy and blend for another 20 seconds. Strain and use to make the purple rainbow dumpling wrappers.

Make the filling: Preheat your oven to 350°F (180°C) and line a baking sheet with parchment paper. Cut the eggplant into small cubes and place into a medium bowl. In a small bowl, combine the remaining filling ingredients and whisk until well mixed. Add the mixture to the eggplant and toss until well coated. Spread evenly on the prepared baking sheet and roast for 30 minutes, stirring halfway through. Remove from the oven and let cool.

Working with 1 dumpling wrapper at a time, place 1 heaping tablespoon (20 g) of filling in the center of a wrapper and shape into a triangle shape (see page 144). Cover loosely with a clean, damp tea towel and repeat the process to form the remaining dumplings.

Cook the dumplings: In a large nonstick skillet with a lid, heat 1 tablespoon (15 ml) of vegetable oil over medium-high heat. Working in batches, add the dumplings, pleated side up. Press down firmly to flatten their base and cook, uncovered, until the base is golden brown, about 3 minutes. Add ½ cup (120 ml) of water to the pan and cover with the lid. Cook for 5 to 7 minutes. Remove the lid and continue to cook until the liquid has cooked off and the undersides of the dumplings are crisp again. If needed, add more oil to help crisp them up. Serve with Black Vinegar and Tamari and top with sliced chives.

BLACK: BLACK COD AND CHIVE DUMPLINGS

Black cod (a.k.a. sablefish) is a much softer and slightly fattier alternative to your standard cod, but standard cod is just fine in this recipe, too, if you can't find black cod! I know this chapter is supposed to be deriving the health from naturally occurring foods, but fat and oil carry flavor impeccably. Besides, the activated charcoal used to pigment the endless dark black wrapper of this dumpling is commonly used as a health supplement to help cleanse your body of toxins! If you can't find activated charcoal, squid ink will make a fine (and healthy) substitute instead.

Like the miso black cod made famous by Nobu, this recipe uses black cod for the same impression of luxury and richness of flavor. Make this for a special occasion, as guests will feel spoiled by this lavish dumpling. Everything, from the dark, shiny appearance of the dumplings themselves to the delicate filling, exudes elegance.

MAKES 24 DUMPLINGS

Colored Wrappers

6 tbsp + 2 tsp (100 ml) water

1 tsp activated charcoal powder

24 black Rainbow Dumpling Wrappers (page 142)

Filling

10½ oz (300 g) black cod

½ tsp salt

Pinch of ground white pepper

¼ cup (60 ml) chicken stock

5 tsp (25 ml) light soy sauce

1 tbsp (15 ml) Shaoxing rice wine

2 tbsp (30 ml) vegetable oil

5 tsp (25 ml) sesame oil

3 tbsp (25 g) finely grated fresh ginger

¾ cup (36 g) chopped Chinese chives

Vegetable oil, for frying

Tobiko (fish roe), for serving

Roasted Sichuan Chile Oil (page 130), for serving

Make the colored wrappers: In a blender, combine the water and activated charcoal powder and blend until smooth. Use to make black rainbow dumpling wrappers.

Make the filling: Cut the fish into ¾-inch (2-cm) cubes. In a food processor, combine the fish with the salt, white pepper, chicken stock, light soy sauce, Shaoxing rice wine, vegetable oil and sesame oil. Pulse until a coarse paste is formed. Transfer the paste to a medium bowl and mix in the ginger and Chinese chives. Cover and let rest in the fridge for at least 30 minutes.

Working with 1 dumpling wrapper at a time, place 1 heaping tablespoon (20 g) of filling in the center of a wrapper and shape into a crescent moon shape (see page 147). Cover loosely with a clean, damp tea towel and repeat the process to form the remaining dumplings.

Cook the dumplings: In a large nonstick skillet with a lid, heat 1 tablespoon (15 ml) of vegetable oil over medium-high heat. Working in batches, add the dumplings, pleated side up. Press down firmly to flatten their base and cook, uncovered, until the base is golden brown, about 3 minutes. Add ½ cup (120 ml) of water to the pan and cover with the lid. Cook for 5 to 7 minutes. Remove the lid and continue to cook until the liquid has cooked off and the undersides of the dumplings are crisp again. If needed, add more oil to help crisp them up.

Serve with tobiko and Roasted Sichuan Chile Oil.

FIVE

BUNS, RICE AND NOODLES

Many of the dishes in this chapter, such as the BBQ Pork Steamed Buns (page 91), made their way here from the dim sum table. Buns and bao are not quite dumplings, but are a similar enough dough + filling concept that holds a place in my heart, and are absolutely worthy of having their own section. Although bao buns can be a bit more of a side dish or accompaniment, a lot of the other dishes in this chapter make the perfect addition to have with some bao buns.

Having said that, alongside these buns and bao are some of my favorite stand-alones that I've had regularly at my dinner table, such as the Special Crab Fried Rice (page 99), or some that I've taken a liking to and put my own twist on, such as the BBQ Pork and Crispy Wonton Noodles (page 103). None of these favorites will be as glorious as I make them out to be without a good wok—the smoky element adds another dimension that changes these from your run-of-the-mill Chinese restaurant standard dish into a real blockbuster.

As for some of the other dishes, in my opinion, they're all the perfect accompaniment to have with dumplings and, well, they're just too good not to share! For me, some were the true introduction into the different flavor profiles and ingredients that reflect the diverse and rich subcultures in all the different regions throughout China. Spicy Dan Dan Noodles (page 104), for example, was a baptism of fire into the Sichuan province and its cuisine, and after making this for my family one day, these mind-blowing noodles opened up my curiosity into other signature regional dishes.

These dishes are all here because they have some of the best signature flavors, are iconic dishes in Chinese cuisine and are each the perfect thing to feast on with a side of any dumplings. They're all dishes I've been exposed to over the journey of food that is my life, so at different stages, from childhood to adulthood, they have all found a special place in my heart—and now I get to share this fondness with everyone!

FRIED CHICKEN BAO BUNS

Who doesn't like fried chicken?

This is a good place to start if you're beginning to work with the classic bao bun dough. Instead of getting a handle on the right mix of fillings wrapped nicely in a neat bun, these bao buns are simply folded in half on themselves after the first proofing, then just fill them like a taco when they're ready to go.

Here, crispy fried chicken meets a pillowy steamed bun. Load these bao buns heavily with chiles, pickles, fresh cilantro and some spicy Korean gochujang mayonnaise.

MAKES 10 TO 12 BAO BUNS

Pickled Carrot

2 carrots, julienned

1 cup (240 ml) pickling liquid (page 108)

Gochujang Aioli

1 tbsp (20 g) gochujang (Korean chili paste)

6 tbsp (84 g) Kewpie brand or regular mayonnaise

½ clove garlic, crushed (optional)

Fried Chicken

6 boneless chicken thighs, cut in half crosswise

1 tbsp (15 ml) soy sauce

2 tsp (12 g) salt, plus more for sprinkling

2 tsp (9 g) superfine sugar

1 tsp sesame oil

½ tsp Chinese five-spice powder

1 tsp minced garlic

1 tsp minced fresh ginger

1 cup (130 g) cornstarch

¼ cup (30 g) all-purpose flour

2 tbsp (20 g) white rice flour

Pinch of salt

Vegetable oil, for frying

Make the pickled carrot: In a medium nonreactive bowl, combine the carrot and pickling liquid. Cover and refrigerate for anywhere between 3 and 24 hours, or until needed.

Make the gochujang aioli: In a small bowl, stir together the gochujang, mayonnaise and garlic. Cover and refrigerate until needed.

Make the fried chicken: In a large bowl, combine the chicken thigh pieces with the soy sauce, salt, sugar, sesame oil, Chinese five-spice powder, garlic and ginger and mix to coat well. Cover and refrigerate for at least 3 hours to marinate.

(continued)

FRIED CHICKEN BAO BUNS (CONT.)

2⅓ cups (320 g) cake flour, plus more for dusting

1 tsp instant yeast

1 tbsp (13 g) superfine sugar

½ cup + 2 tbsp (150 ml) milk, plus more if needed

1 tbsp (15 ml) vegetable oil, plus more for brushing

Pinch of salt

Fresh cilantro, for garnish

Sliced red chile peppers, for garnish

Make the bao bun dough: In a separate large bowl, combine the cake flour, instant yeast and sugar. If you are using a stand mixer, attach the dough hook and turn on at low speed. Slowly pour in the milk and oil. If the dough is a little dry, add more milk a tablespoon (15 ml) at a time until the dough comes together. Increase the speed to medium and knead for 5 minutes. Alternatively, if you are kneading the dough by hand, this will take about 10 minutes. Once the dough is smooth, add a pinch of salt and knead for an additional 2 minutes, or until combined and smooth again. Wrap the dough with plastic wrap and let rest for 20 minutes.

Shape the dough into a 1¼-inch (3-cm)-thick log and cut it into 10 to 12 equal pieces. Roll each piece into a ball and allow them to rest for 3 minutes. Roll out each ball to about ⅛ inch (3 to 4 mm) thick and use a 4-inch (10-cm)-diameter round cookie cutter to trim into circles. Lightly brush the surface of the rolled-out dough with oil and gently fold in half. Transfer to a baking sheet lined with parchment paper and cover with a clean, damp tea towel. Let the dough rise at room temperature until doubled in size, about 1 hour.

Cook the fried chicken: In a medium bowl, stir together the cornstarch, all-purpose flour, rice flour and a pinch of salt. In a large, deep saucepan, heat the vegetable oil to 350°F (180°C). Test by dipping a wooden chopstick into the oil: The chopstick will sizzle when the oil is ready. Coat the chicken in the flour mixture and gently lower into the oil. Cook until golden brown, 4 to 6 minutes. Drain on a baking sheet lined with paper towels and sprinkle with a little extra salt.

Now that all components are ready, we can now cook the bao buns. Line a bamboo steamer with parchment paper and place in a wok. Pour enough water into the wok for the water line to be 1 inch (2.5 cm) below the bottom of the steamer. Place the buns 1 inch (2.5 cm) apart in the steamer basket to allow for them to expand. Steam over low heat for 8 to 10 minutes.

Once the buns are cooked, split them open and gently fill with the fried chicken, gochujang aioli, pickled carrot, cilantro and sliced chiles. Serve immediately.

NOTES

You can use active dry yeast, but make sure to rehydrate the yeast in water or milk with 1 teaspoon of superfine sugar.

The cake flour can be replaced with 1¾ cups + 4 teaspoons (225 g) of all-purpose flour plus ⅓ cup (45 g) of cornstarch.

BIANG BIANG NOODLES WITH SPICY CUMIN LAMB

Many of the ingredients used in this dish are featured in most of the other recipes in this book, except for two: lamb and cumin. Lamb is used sparingly throughout Chinese cuisine, but really finds its home in the north of China. The same goes for cumin. Cumin has a powerful nutty flavor that marries happily with coriander, but goes especially well with gamey meats like lamb.

Cumin is the major player in these noodles from Central-Northern China. Toast your spices first in a dry wok to really amp up the flavor and toastiness as well as bring out the signature nuttiness of the cumin.

Making the noodles themselves is supereasy! No intricate wrapping or preparation required—just roll out your dough and cut the noodles by hand, nice and thick—it works better if they're irregular and uneven!

SERVES 4

Noodles

3 cups minus 1 scant tbsp (365 g) all-purpose flour, plus more for dusting

Pinch of salt

⅔ cup minus 1 tsp (155 ml) water, plus more if needed

Vegetable oil, for coating

Dash of sesame oil

Lamb Mixture

14 oz (400 g) fatty lamb shoulder, sliced

¼ cup (60 ml) vegetable oil, divided

3 tbsp (45 ml) Shaoxing rice wine, divided

1 tsp cornstarch

1 tbsp (6 g) cumin seeds, toasted

2 tsp (4 g) coriander seeds, toasted

Pinch of ground white pepper

Make the noodles: In the bowl of a stand mixer fitted with the dough hook attachment, combine the flour and salt. Starting on low speed, slowly incorporate the water. If the dough is a little dry, add another tablespoon (15 ml) of water at a time. Increase the speed to medium and let knead for 10 to 15 minutes, or until smooth and elastic. Cover with plastic wrap and let rest for 1 hour.

Line a baking sheet with parchment paper and set aside. Brush a clean work surface with vegetable oil and press the dough into a ½-inch (1.3-cm)-thick rectangle. Cut into 10 to 12 equal strips, laying them flat on the oiled surface. Pick up 1 noodle by both ends and lift it while slapping it repeatedly onto the work surface as you stretch it to a ribbon that is about 8 inches (20 cm) long. Place your noodle on the prepared baking sheet and repeat the process. Cover with plastic wrap to prevent drying out and set aside until needed.

Prepare the lamb: In a medium bowl, combine the lamb, 1 tablespoon (15 ml) of the vegetable oil, 1 tablespoon (15 ml) of the Shaoxing rice wine and the cornstarch. Toss well and set aside to marinate for at least 30 minutes.

In a mortar and pestle, grind the cumin seeds, coriander seeds and ground white pepper together and set aside until needed.

(continued)

BIANG BIANG NOODLES
WITH SPICY CUMIN LAMB (CONT.)

2½ tbsp (20 g) finely grated fresh ginger

2 green onions, white part only, chopped

1 small head garlic, minced

1 red chile pepper, sliced

3 tbsp (45 ml) Roasted Sichuan Chile Oil (page 130)

1 tsp superfine sugar

1 tsp Chinese black vinegar

1 tbsp (15 ml) soy sauce

Pinch of salt

1 red onion, thinly sliced

3 heads bok choy, cut into chunks

1 bunch cilantro, separated into leaves and finely sliced stalks

1 tbsp (8 g) sesame seeds, toasted

Chopped cilantro, for garnish

Roasted Sichuan Chile Oil (page 130), for serving

Cook the noodles: Bring a large pot of salted water to a boil. Cook the noodles for 2 to 3 minutes, or until they rise to the surface. Drain and transfer to a bowl. Toss with a dash of sesame oil to stop them from sticking.

Heat a large wok over medium heat and add the remaining 3 tablespoons (45 ml) of vegetable oil followed by the ginger and green onions. Cook, stirring, for 1 minute before adding the garlic and chile. Cook for an additional 30 seconds. Increase the heat to high and add the lamb. Stir-fry until just browned, then add the remaining 2 tablespoons (30 ml) of Shaoxing rice wine, the spice mixture, the chile oil, sugar, black vinegar, soy sauce, salt, red onion and bok choy. Cook until the bok choy is just cooked but still crunchy. Add the cooked noodles, cilantro and toasted sesame seeds. Toss gently before serving.

Serve with chopped cilantro and Roasted Sichuan Chile Oil, as desired.

BBQ PORK STEAMED BUNS

At lunchtime in any city's Chinatown district, there's a long queue of empty stomachs just waiting for some BBQ pork steamed buns (char siu bao) from the dim sum trolley, just like the queues waiting for a table. Some claim dim sum dates back to no more than 16 centuries ago, but the earliest record we have is from the 10th century China, where it literally means "to lightly touch the heart." The heart of this dish comes from the sticky red pork inside the fluffy white steamed buns. Chinese five-spice powder and hoisin in the pork's marinade give it the spicy-sweet flavor that makes char siu pork a classic staple of Chinese food—but save yourself time by making it one day in advance.

MAKES 10 TO 12 BUNS

BBQ Pork Filling

1 tbsp (8 g) cornstarch

6 tbsp + 2 tsp (100 ml) water

1 tbsp (15 ml) vegetable oil, for frying

½ red onion, finely chopped

1 tbsp (15 ml) light soy sauce

1 tbsp (15 ml) oyster sauce

1 tbsp (15 ml) hoisin sauce

½ tsp Chinese five-spice powder

2 tsp (10 ml) sesame oil

1 tbsp (13 g) superfine sugar

2 cups (350 g) finely diced Chinese BBQ pork (char siu), store-bought

Bao bun dough (page 86)

Make the filling: In a small bowl, mix the cornstarch with the water and set aside for 2 minutes.

In a wok, heat the oil over medium-high heat and add the onion. Cook, stirring, for 1 minute. Lower the heat to medium-low, then add the cornstarch slurry, light soy sauce, oyster sauce, hoisin sauce, Chinese five-spice powder, sesame oil and sugar. Cook, stirring, until the mixture bubbles and thickens, about 3 minutes. Remove from the heat and stir in the diced Chinese BBQ pork. Let the filling cool slightly before covering and refrigerating it for at least 30 minutes.

Fill the pork buns: Shape the dough into a 1¼-inch (3-cm)-thick log and cut into 10 to 12 equal pieces. Roll each piece into a ball and allow to rest for 3 minutes. Flatten the dough with the palm of your hand and then, using a rolling pin, roll each piece into a circle 4 to 5 inches (10 to 12.5 cm) in diameter, with a slightly thicker center to help support the filling. Fill a circle of dough with 2 heaping tablespoons (40 g) of the filling. Gather the sides and enclose the filling, pinching to seal and flipping so the seam side is at the bottom. Place the bun onto an individual square piece of parchment paper and continue the process with the remaining dough and filling.

Cook the pork buns: Pour enough water into a wok for the water line to be 1 inch (2.5 cm) below the bottom of a bamboo basket steamer. Place the wok over high heat. Once the water is boiling, steam the buns (on their papers) in batches for 12 minutes. Serve immediately.

NOTE

Using your palms, cup the dough and rotate in a circular motion to shape it taller. This will ensure your bun does not spread to the side after steaming.

PORK AND GARLIC CHIVE BAOZI

If BBQ Pork Steamed Buns (page 91) are the yin, then these baozi are the yang. Instead of the rich sweetness of char siu, there's a more lifted, salty and savory flavor brought out of the pork with the green onions and garlic chives. But although these are polar opposites of the pork buns, they won't go astray together in a bamboo steamer.

The double proofing for the dough means you're in for a little wait till they rise to size; however, these easy-to-make buns are so worth the extra time! Salt the cabbage before you add it to the filling, let it sweat and drain the excess water to get a nice, well-bound filling.

Make sure to have these with some Black Vinegar and Tamari dressing (page 133)!

MAKES 10 TO 12 BUNS

Pork and Garlic Chive Filling

18 oz (510 g) fatty ground pork

2½ tbsp (20 g) finely grated fresh ginger

¼ cup (12 g) finely chopped garlic chives

¼ cup (25 g) finely chopped green onion

Pinch of salt

Pinch of ground white pepper

1 tsp superfine sugar

2 tbsp (30 ml) light soy sauce

1 tbsp (15 ml) Shaoxing rice wine

1 tbsp (15 ml) sesame oil

Bao bun dough (page 86)

Vegetable oil, for frying

Black sesame seeds, for garnish

Black Vinegar and Tamari, (page 133), for serving

Make the filling: In a large bowl, combine all the filling ingredients and mix vigorously in one direction until the mixture binds. Cover and let rest in the fridge for 30 minutes.

Fill the pork buns: Shape the dough into a 1¼-inch (3-cm)-thick log and cut into 10 to 12 equal pieces. Roll each piece into a ball and allow to rest for 3 minutes. Flatten the dough with the palm of your hand and then, using a rolling pin, roll into a circle 4 to 5 inches (10 to 12.5 cm) in diameter, with a slightly thicker center to help support the filling. Fill a circle of dough with 2 heaping tablespoons (40 g) of the filling. Gather the sides and enclose the bun, pinching to seal and flipping so the seam side is at the bottom. Continue the process with the remaining dough and filling.

Cook the pork buns: In a wok, arrange the buns in a single layer. Pour in about 1 tablespoon (15 ml) oil and enough water to cover one-third of the bun. Cover and cook over high heat until the water evaporates and the bottoms of the buns are golden brown, 8 to 10 minutes. Remove the buns from the pan and sprinkle with black sesame seeds. Serve immediately with Black Vinegar and Tamari.

STICKY RICE WRAPPED IN LOTUS LEAF

Lotus flowers are very sacred flowers in many Asian cultures and should be on hand at any good Asian supermarket. Sweet Chinese sausage (lap cheong) and rich Chinese bacon (lap yuk), earthy mushrooms and a slight bitterness from the perfume-y lotus leaves balance out the natural sweetness of the glutinous rice. Steaming draws out all of these flavors into the rice—yum!

MAKES 4 PARCELS

----

2 cups (370 g) uncooked sticky rice

Marinated Chicken

10½ oz (300 g) skinless, boneless chicken thighs, thinly sliced

½ tsp cornstarch

1 tsp vegetable oil

1 tsp oyster sauce

1 tsp Shaoxing rice wine

1 tsp dark soy sauce

Pinch of superfine sugar

Pinch of ground white pepper

Pinch of salt

Rice Seasoning

1 tsp Shaoxing rice wine

1 tsp sesame oil

1 tsp oyster sauce

2 tsp (10 ml) dark soy sauce

Lotus Leaf Parcels

2 dried lotus leaves

2 tbsp (10 g) dried shrimp (optional)

8 dried shiitake mushroom caps

Vegetable oil, for frying

2 medium cloves garlic, minced

1 shallot, minced

3½ oz (100 g) Chinese bacon, sliced

2 (1.75-oz [50-g]) Chinese sausages, thinly sliced

Roasted Sichuan Chile Oil (page 130), for serving

Soak the rice: Place the sticky rice in a large bowl, cover with water and let soak for at least 2 hours. Meanwhile, marinate the chicken: In a medium bowl, combine all the chicken ingredients and stir until well combined. Cover and refrigerate for at least 2 hours. Make the rice seasoning: In a small bowl, stir together all the seasoning ingredients until well combined. Set aside until needed.

In preparation for making the parcels, soak the lotus leaves: Cut each lotus leaf in half down the middle before placing in a container filled with water. Place a plate on top of the leaves to weigh them down and soak for at least 1 hour. If using, soak the dried shrimp in water for 5 minutes, then drain, rinse and pat dry. Drain the sticky rice and transfer to a large bowl along with the dried shrimp. In a separate bowl, rehydrate the shiitake mushrooms in hot water for 15 minutes. Drain, squeeze dry and thinly slice.

Place a wok over high heat and add about 1 tablespoon (15 ml) of vegetable oil. Add the garlic and shallot and cook, stirring constantly, until soft, about 1 minute. Add the shiitake mushrooms and cook until golden brown, about 2 minutes. Transfer the mixture to the sticky rice and stir to combine. Pour in the rice seasoning and stir well to combine. In the same wok, heat an additional tablespoon (15 ml) of vegetable oil over high heat. Add the chicken and cook, stirring, until just cooked through, about 3 minutes. Remove from the wok and transfer to a bowl.

Form the parcels: Drain the lotus leaves, pat dry with towels and arrange them on a work surface. Place ½ cup (100 g) of the sticky rice mixture in the center of each lotus leaf. Top each with one-quarter of the cooked chicken, Chinese bacon and Chinese sausage, followed by another ½ cup (100 g) of sticky rice mixture, spreading it to cover the meat. Wrap each parcel by folding in the edges around the filling to form a tight parcel and, using kitchen twine, tie each up securely.

Line a bamboo steamer with parchment paper and place in a wok. Pour enough water into the wok for the water line to be 1 inch (2.5 cm) below the bottom of the steamer. Place the wok over high heat. Once the water is boiling, place the parcels in the basket and steam for 1½ hours, checking the water level and topping it up to ensure the pan does not dry out. Once cooked, cut off the twine and discard. Serve immediately with Roasted Sichuan Chile Oil.

CLASSIC CHINESE FRIED RICE

Fried rice is one of those dishes that every family has, no matter what their cultural background is. For many families, fried rice is an easy-to-make comfort dish and a good way to throw in unused vegetables with some leftover rice, and my family is no different.

Add whatever veggies you like, but I prefer to keep this simple—shrimp, green onions, garlic, Chinese sausage (lap cheong) and plenty of scrambled egg. The lap cheong makes this for me but can always be swapped out for bacon (most fridges are stocked with some). After all, this is about getting rid of leftovers!

SERVES 6

----

3 (1.75-oz [50-g]) lap cheong (Chinese sausages)

Rice Seasoning

Pinch of salt

Pinch of ground white pepper

Pinch of superfine sugar

½ tsp sesame oil

1 tsp soy sauce

½ tsp dark soy sauce

2 tsp (10 ml) hot water

5 tbsp (75 ml) vegetable oil, for frying, divided

2 large eggs, beaten

2 cloves garlic, minced

5 oz (150 g) raw shrimp, chopped

1 medium onion, chopped

5 cups (930 g) cold cooked white rice

1 cup (100 g) mung bean sprouts

2 green onions, chopped

Prepare the lap cheong by steaming it on a heatproof plate in a steamer basket over boiling water for 20 minutes, or until the sausages are translucent. Cut into diagonal slices and set aside until needed.

Make the rice seasoning: In a small bowl, stir together all the ingredients until well combined. Set aside until needed.

Heat your wok over high heat and add 2 tablespoons (30 ml) of the vegetable oil. Add the beaten eggs and scramble by breaking up into smaller pieces with a spatula. Once the scrambled eggs are just cooked, remove the eggs and transfer them to a bowl; set aside until needed.

Keeping your wok over high heat, add another 2 tablespoons (30 ml) of vegetable oil. Add the garlic and stir until fragrant, about 2 minutes. Add the shrimp and stir-fry until just cooked, about 2 minutes. Remove the shrimp mixture and transfer into a bowl; set aside until needed.

Lower the heat to medium and add the last tablespoon (15 ml) of vegetable oil. Add the sliced Chinese sausage and stir-fry for 20 seconds. Add the chopped onion and stir-fry until translucent, about 2 minutes. Increase the heat to high and add the rice. Use your spatula to flatten the rice and break up any clumps. Once the rice is warmed, pour the seasoning mixture evenly over the rice and toss until well coated. Add the scrambled egg, shrimp, bean sprouts and green onions and toss for an additional minute, or until well combined. Serve immediately.

SPECIAL CRAB FRIED RICE

Grandmère used to make this for my brother and me all the time while we were growing up; so many fond memories come with making and eating this twist on fried rice. It actually has very few elements but is still so tasty! All the flavor comes from the aromatics, and the hot wok that gets the rice nice and smoky but never overpowers the crabmeat. Hold off on adding in leftovers and embark on the journey to get everything you need (if you can). Simplicity is the key. The chile and garlic sauce gives a piquant contrast to the smoky rice—add a drizzle or go wild like I do.

Whip up some Grandmère's Boxing Chicken (page 124) for your rice, too, if you wish. That's how Grandmère used to make it for me, and there's not much fried chicken can't make even better.

SERVES 4

Chile and Garlic Dipping Sauce

¼ cup (60 ml) white vinegar

Pinch of salt

½ tsp superfine sugar

1 to 2 red bird's eye chiles, finely chopped

1 medium clove garlic, finely grated

Fried Rice

3 to 4 tbsp (45 to 60 ml) vegetable oil

6 tbsp (50 g) finely grated fresh ginger

2 cloves garlic, minced

2 green onions, chopped, divided

4 cups (745 g) cold cooked short-grain rice

Pinch of ground white pepper

Pinch of superfine sugar

3 tbsp (45 ml) light soy sauce

Salt

2 large eggs, beaten

2 tbsp (70 g) finely chopped preserved mustard greens

1 cup (140 g) cooked crabmeat

Handful of chopped fresh cilantro, plus more for serving

Make the dipping sauce: In a small bowl, stir together all the sauce ingredients until the sugar has dissolved and the mixture is well combined. Cover and refrigerate until needed.

Make the fried rice: In a wok, heat the oil over medium-high heat. Add the ginger and cook, stirring, for 30 seconds, followed by the garlic and one of the green onions. Stir-fry for an additional 30 seconds, or until aromatic. Add the rice, increase the heat to high and toss with a spatula to combine. Use your spatula to flatten the rice and break up any clumps. Add the white pepper, sugar and light soy sauce. Toss and season with salt to taste.

Using your spatula, spread out the rice into an even layer along the surface of the wok. Pour the beaten egg evenly over the rice and stir until all the egg is cooked and broken into pieces. Add the preserved mustard greens and crab and toss until combined and the crab is warmed. Add the remaining green onion and cilantro and toss until well combined. Serve immediately with the dipping sauce and additional cilantro.

CANTONESE CHICKEN AND SALTED FISH FRIED RICE

Salted fish is a pretty scary element to bring into the kitchen, but do not be afraid! I promise it is the hero of this dish. Whereas the Special Crab Fried Rice (page 99) is light and fragrant, this fried rice is rich and salty.

First, talk to your Asian grocer for help getting "Chinese-style salted fish"—the last thing you want is to end up with some horrible canned salty fish.

Second, use chicken thighs, not breasts—the flavor that comes from rendering the fat from the thighs puts a nice rich base through the rice.

Third, don't be shy of the salted fish, but don't go crazy—a little goes a long way.

SERVES 4

- -

¼ cup (60 ml) vegetable oil, for frying, divided

1 oz (30 g) salted fish, or to taste, skinned and lightly rinsed in water (see note)

3½ oz (100 g) skinless, boneless chicken thighs, cut into small cubes

2 large eggs, beaten

Salt

4 cups (630 g) cold cooked long-grain white rice

2 green onions, thinly sliced

1 cup (100 g) mung bean sprouts

1 tbsp (15 ml) light soy sauce

1 tsp Shaoxing rice wine

1 tsp sesame oil

Freshly ground black pepper

Place a wok over high heat and add 2 tablespoons (30 ml) of vegetable oil. Add the salted fish and stir-fry until golden and crisp, 2 to 3 minutes. Remove from the wok, using a slotted spoon, and transfer to a bowl. Set aside until needed. Add the chicken to the wok and cook, stirring constantly, until white and just cooked through, 4 to 6 minutes. Remove from the wok with a slotted spoon and transfer to a separate bowl. Set aside until needed.

Add another 2 tablespoons (30 ml) of vegetable oil to the wok, followed by the beaten eggs and a pinch of salt. Swirl your wok to evenly coat with the eggs. When just set, add the rice and, with your spatula, toss to combine and separate any grains that are clumped together. Add the salted fish, chicken, green onions, bean sprouts, light soy sauce, Shaoxing rice wine and sesame oil. Season to taste with salt and black pepper. Toss to combine and serve immediately.

NOTE

Ask your local Asian grocer for Nan Fong's salted fish.

BBQ PORK AND CRISPY WONTON NOODLES

As opposed to the classic BBQ pork with egg noodles in broth, these dry noodles are A-grade comfort food that most with Chinese backgrounds will know immediately. This is a solid street vendor or food court dish that's so easy to grab while you're out, in a rush and on the cheap—why not dress it up and make it really something?

Choy sum (a relative of Chinese broccoli; any Chinese leafy green may be substituted) helps break this up a bit so it's not all fried noodles and sweet pork. My variation adds in Grandmère's Fried Shrimp Wontons (page 56), too, for some added crunch.

SERVES 4

Pickled Green Chiles

⅔ cup (160 ml) white vinegar

½ tsp salt

3 tbsp (39 g) superfine sugar

6 long green chiles, thinly sliced

Shallot Oil

6 tbsp (90 ml) vegetable oil

3 shallots, finely sliced

Sauce

2 tbsp (30 ml) dark soy sauce

1 tsp light soy sauce

1 tsp sweet soy sauce

½ tsp salt

½ tsp superfine sugar

1 tsp sesame oil

14 oz (400 g) uncooked wonton noodles (egg noodles)

1 bunch choy sum (see above), trimmed

Chinese BBQ pork (char siu), store-bought, for serving

Grandmère's Fried Shrimp Wontons (page 56), for serving

Make the pickled green chiles: In a medium nonreactive bowl, stir together the vinegar, salt and sugar until the sugar has dissolved. Place the sliced chiles into a separate heatproof, nonreactive bowl and pour boiling water to cover them. Let stand for 30 seconds before draining. Pour the vinegar solution over the chiles and refrigerate for at least 2 hours.

Make the shallot oil: In a medium skillet, heat the vegetable oil over medium heat. Once hot, add the shallots and cook, stirring, for 5 to 7 minutes, or until golden brown. Remove from the heat and set aside. Reserve ¼ cup (60 ml) of the oil and keep any remaining shallot oil for serving.

Make the sauce: In a small bowl, stir together all the sauce ingredients plus the ¼ cup (60 ml) of reserved shallot oil. Set the sauce aside.

Cook the noodles: Bring a large pot of salted water to a boil and cook the noodles for 2 to 3 minutes, or until they rise to the surface. Drain and transfer to a bowl. Mix in the sauce and toss to coat. Portion out the noodles onto four plates.

In a fresh pot of boiling salted water, blanch the choy sum for 15 seconds, or until just cooked. Portion onto the plates of noodles followed by a drizzle of the remaining shallot oil. Top the noodles with your desired amount of Chinese BBQ pork, a few of Grandmère's Fried Shrimp Wontons and some pickled green chiles. Serve immediately.

SPICY DAN DAN NOODLES

This is a Sichuan favorite that follows through on the Sichuan promise of heat. It's quite spicy, so have some soy milk on standby. Shredded fatty pork, sesame paste, Sichuan peppercorns, homemade roasted chile oil, preserved mustard greens (*siu mi ya cai*)—I love this dish so much for its complexity and intensity.

The preserved mustard greens are kind of funky and kind of tangy, and for me that's what makes these noodles so distinct. The layering of the dish doesn't stop at the flavor but follows through to plating up. Drop the noodles into the sauce—very similar to the Bang Bang Sauce (page 137)—then, chuck in the leafy greens, fried pork and preserved greens and condiments and toss!

SERVES 4

Meat Mixture

2 tbsp (30 ml) vegetable oil, divided

8 oz (225 g) fatty ground pork

2 tsp (10 ml) hoisin sauce

2 tsp (10 ml) Shaoxing rice wine

1 tsp dark soy sauce

½ tsp Chinese five-spice powder

5 tbsp (18 g) preserved mustard greens

Dan Dan Sauce

2 tbsp (30 ml) tahini

3 tbsp (45 ml) light soy sauce

2 tsp (9 g) superfine sugar

½ tsp ground Sichuan pepper

½ cup (120 ml) Roasted Sichuan Chile Oil (page 130)

2 cloves garlic, minced

1 lb (450 g) fresh medium-thickness white noodles

1 bunch choy sum (see page 103), trimmed

Chopped roasted peanuts, for serving

Chopped green onion, for serving

1 cup (240 ml) Roasted Sichuan Chile Oil (page 130)

Make the meat mixture: In a wok over medium heat, heat 1 tablespoon (15 ml) of the vegetable oil. Add the pork and cook, stirring constantly, until cooked through and browned, about 5 minutes. Add the hoisin sauce, Shaoxing rice wine, dark soy sauce and Chinese five-spice powder. Cook, stirring, until the liquid has evaporated. Remove from the heat and transfer to a bowl. Return the wok to the heat and add the remaining tablespoon (15 ml) of vegetable oil followed by the preserved mustard greens. Sauté for 3 to 5 minutes, or until lightly browned and fragrant before transferring to a small bowl. Set both the pork mixture and the preserved greens aside until needed.

Make the sauce: In a bowl, stir together all the sauce ingredients until well combined. Season to taste and loosen with hot water, if needed.

Cook the noodles: Bring a large pot of salted water to a boil and cook the noodles for 2 to 3 minutes, or until they rise to the surface. Blanch the choy sum separately and drain.

To serve, divide the sauce among four bowls, followed by the noodles, choy sum, cooked pork, preserved mustard greens, chopped peanuts and green onion and top generously with Roasted Sichuan Chile Oil. Serve immediately, instructing your guests to toss, to ensure all the flavors are well combined.

SIX

APPETIZERS AND SNACKS

After you've been slaving away in the kitchen making the most perfect dumplings, you deserve to catch a break somewhere, so I've deliberately tried to keep this chapter simple—it's not all about fine dining! I begin to bring in some new techniques in these little additions and sides, but don't be alarmed—they're still supereasy to throw together quickly!

The Salt and Pepper Silken Tofu (page 116) introduces you to "crusting" your protein with nonwheat flours as an alternative to a heavy batter. So much time and cleanup can be saved by using this method, and the crispy crust it yields is incredible. Although "crusting" makes a reappearance with Fried Squid Tentacles (page 120) and Grandmère's Boxing Chicken (page 124), their marinades do involve some waiting time. This is unavoidable but with a little preparation, the actual time in the kitchen will be minimized, and this is very forgiving to those with busy lifestyles, like me!

Having friends and family over for dinner and putting on an amazing spread is one of my favorite things to do! The excited feeling I get from covering the dinner table in a feast of different things and seeing everyone's eyes bulge is like no other. But that kind of thing takes a bit of planning and is not always easy to do on the fly . . . or is it?

Daily, I juggle running my dumpling kitchen (Bumplings), working on a bunch of other side projects and making time to keep fit and healthy, so I've had to learn the little hacks to pump out impressive recipes on the fly and with little preparation. Now, I'm going to share them with you!

This chapter is about creating a wholesome Chinese meal on the quick! Smacked Cucumber Salad (page 111) or Sesame Shrimp Toasts (page 112) are an easy way to trick out any Chinese dish, or even some leftover Chinese takeout. There are some good menu fatteners in here, so instead of spending hours in the kitchen for a mammoth dinner, save some time, turn your meal into a feast and blow away all your dinner guests!

CHINESE PICKLED RADISH

Chinese pickled radish is a refreshing, sweet and sour condiment that I always keep at home in the fridge. It's something I like to snack on but also serve as part of a starter to help cleanse the palate. These pickles are also great to help cut through fatty dishes, hence they go very well with Grandmère's Boxing Chicken (page 124).

Make a whole jar's worth and set it aside for the future—a worthy long-term investment. Napa cabbage is the stock standard for a pickle, but my preference is to use a combination of daikon radish and red radish, which results in something a little crunchier! Leave a bit of space in whatever you pickle them in—the longer you pickle, the more the veggies expand, and you'll need some space to keep topping them up with boiled water.

SERVES 8

---

21 oz (600 g) daikon radishes

21 oz (600 g) red radishes

3 tbsp (54 g) salt

3 cloves garlic, minced

3 long red chiles, sliced

Pickling Liquid

2 cups + 5 tsp (500 ml) water

1 cup (200 g) superfine sugar

1 cup (240 ml) white vinegar

½ tsp salt, plus more if desired

Roasted Sichuan Chile Oil (page 130), for serving

Fried garlic flakes, for garnish

Prepare the radishes: Trim off and discard the leafy green top from the daikon radishes and shave the outside with a vegetable peeler. Cut into ¾-inch (2-cm) cubes and place in a medium bowl. Trim off and discard the leafy green tops from the red radishes and cut into quarters. Place the red radish in the same bowl as the daikon radish and add the salt. Using your hands, toss and lightly massage the vegetables with the salt to ensure it is distributed evenly. Cover and refrigerate to marinate for approximately 1 hour. This process helps to remove the liquid from the vegetables and make them crunchy.

Make the pickling liquid: In a medium nonreactive saucepan, combine the water and sugar. Bring to a boil, then turn off the heat. Add the vinegar and salt and stir to combine. Let the liquid cool down to room temperature, then season to taste with more salt, if needed.

Remove the radishes from the fridge and wash a few times to get rid of the salt. Transfer to a lidded nonreactive container. Add the garlic and chiles and pour the pickling liquid over the vegetables. Stir to combine. Cover and refrigerate for 24 hours before serving. Serve with Roasted Sichuan Chile Oil and fried garlic flakes.

> NOTE
>
> Fried garlic flakes can be bought at an Asian specialty store.

SMACKED CUCUMBER SALAD

This is one of my personal favorites. The big aesthetic value in this dish comes from the contrast of the bright green cucumbers with the bright red homemade roasted chile oil. And it has a contrasting palate to match: fresh, cooling cucumber with a spicy, garlicky, tangy dressing. It's delicious, simple, looks impressive and takes no time to make! Goes great on the side with some Spicy Sichuan Pork Wontons (page 30), too. I won't waste too much time describing it—get smashing!

Hot tip: Grab a spoon and scrape out and discard not only the seeds but their surrounding pulp to make the cucumber extra-crunchy.

SERVES 4

- -

10½ oz (300 g) English cucumbers

Cucumber Salad Dressing

3 cloves garlic, minced

4 tsp (20 ml) Chinese black vinegar

4 tsp (20 ml) tamari

1 tsp superfine sugar

½ tsp salt

Dash of sesame oil

Roasted Sichuan Chile Oil (page 130), for serving

White toasted sesame seeds, for garnish

Prepare the cucumbers: Wash well and peel in a zebra pattern, leaving long strips of the green skin intact. Cut the cucumbers lengthwise, then, using a teaspoon, scrape out the seeds. This step is optional, however, I find it helps toward keeping the cucumbers crunchy. Lay the sliced cucumbers face down on a chopping board and, using a cleaver or rolling pin, smack the cucumbers lightly to break it into chunks. Chop coarsely and transfer to a medium bowl.

Make the dressing: In a small bowl, stir together all the sauce ingredients until the sugar is dissolved.

To finish, pour the dressing over the cucumbers and toss well to coat. Drizzle with some Roasted Sichuan Chile Oil and top with toasted white sesame seeds. Serve immediately.

SESAME SHRIMP TOASTS

Shrimp toast is a nice little snack that goes down well for both seafood lovers and those who can't stand it. It's no authentic bite by any means, but this mild seafood snack is definitely a crowd-pleaser. Although not mandatory, refrigerate the shrimp "mousse" for a few hours before lathering up your bread, to get as much of the ginger, garlic and sesame into the shrimp.

If you're in a rush, blitz your shrimp with all the other ingredients and smother each piece of bread in it. Get that wok burning with plenty of oil inside, crust the mousse side with sesame seeds and fry till golden brown. Great way to zhoozh-up the dry end of a bread loaf, or even if you just need a greasy Chinese fix in a stitch.

MAKES 16 PIECES

----

7 oz (200 g) raw shrimp, peeled and deveined

1 large egg white

2½ tbsp (20 g) finely grated fresh ginger

1 tsp light soy sauce

½ tsp superfine sugar

Pinch of salt

Pinch of ground white pepper

1 tbsp (3 g) finely chopped fresh cilantro

4 slices white bread

1 large egg, lightly beaten

⅔ cup (100 g) white sesame seeds

Vegetable oil, for frying

Roasted Sichuan Chile Oil (page 130), for serving

Black Vinegar and Tamari (page 133), for serving

Make the shrimp paste: In a food processor, combine the shrimp, egg white, ginger, light soy sauce, sugar, salt and white pepper and blitz to a paste. Transfer to a medium bowl. Add the chopped cilantro and stir until well combined.

Spread the shrimp paste evenly over the 4 slices of bread. Brush lightly with the beaten egg and pat a layer of sesame seeds onto the toasts. Set the slices of bread aside, shrimp side up, on a baking sheet until ready to cook.

Fry the toasts: In a large, deep skillet, add vegetable oil to a depth of 1¼ inches (3 cm) and heat over high heat. Once hot, fry the sesame shrimp toasts, unspread side down, for about 2 minutes. Carefully turn over onto the shrimp side and cook for 1½ minutes, or until the sesame seeds are golden and the shrimp paste is cooked through. Remove and drain on a baking sheet lined with paper towels. Cut each slice of shrimp toast into quarters to make 16 triangles in total. Serve immediately with Roasted Sichuan Chile Oil and Black Vinegar and Tamari.

GREEN ONION PANCAKE

This is one of the most common and wholesome snacks you can get on the streets of China. One massive green onion pancake (*cong you bing*) goes for around 1 yuan (about 13 cents) on the streets in the homeland, but in any Chinese restaurant in the Western world they go for sometimes 20 times that! Cheaper, better and easy to make at home—guarantees the quality.

This is more like a light, flaky, savory flatbread than a fluffy pancake. No leavening or rising agents are added, just flour. Like the dumpling doughs, it needs to be worked till it shines, then left to rest as you would with pancakes.

Eat with both hands.

SERVES 4

----

2 cups (250 g) all-purpose flour, plus more for dusting

Salt

1 cup (240 ml) warm water

Vegetable oil

1 cup (100 g) thinly sliced green onions, green part only, divided

Black Vinegar and Tamari (page 133), for serving

Make the pancake dough: In a large bowl, stir together the flour and a pinch of salt. Create a well in the center and slowly pour in the warm water while mixing with a fork. Turn out the dough onto a lightly floured surface and knead until smooth and elastic, about 10 minutes. Alternatively, if you are using a stand mixer, the kneading process will take 5 to 6 minutes. Once smooth, transfer the dough to a bowl that has been oiled lightly with vegetable oil, cover with plastic wrap and let rest for 20 minutes.

Divide the dough into 4 equal pieces. Working with one piece at a time, roll out as thinly as possible on a lightly floured surface. Brush with vegetable oil and sprinkle with ¼ cup (25 g) of the sliced green onions. Season with salt and roll the dough away from you to form a long, thin cylinder. Starting at one end, roll the cylinder onto itself in a spiral motion to create a coil. Cover with plastic wrap and repeat with the remaining pieces of dough.

Flatten each coil of dough with the palm of your hand and reroll into a disk. In a saucepan, heat 1 tablespoon (15 ml) of vegetable oil over medium-low heat and, working with one pancake at a time, cook, turning frequently until each side is golden and crisp, about 10 minutes. Transfer to a wire rack and rest for about 5 minutes before cutting into wedges. Serve with Black Vinegar and Tamari.

SALT AND PEPPER SILKEN TOFU

This is so much more than just tofu dusted with salt and pepper—but not by much: There is always "salt and pepper" something at the dinner table when I go out for Chinese food. The secret to this dish is in the cornstarch. The crust the starch gives to the soft tofu once deep-fried is unbelievable: the ultimate contrast in texture.

All the best bits are those small and supercrunchy crumbles of tofu that break off and get left behind in the bottom of the wok. Make it your mission to go back and fish them out!

SERVES 2

Silken Tofu

10½ oz (300 g) silken tofu

½ cup (64 g) cornstarch

1 tsp freshly ground black pepper

1 tsp ground white pepper

½ tsp Chinese five-spice powder

1 tsp salt

2 cups (480 ml) vegetable oil

Spice Mixture

½ tsp salt

½ tsp superfine sugar

¼ tsp ground white pepper

Pinch of Chinese five-spice powder

Pinch of ground Sichuan peppercorns

Roasted Sichuan Chile Oil (page 130), for serving

Make the tofu: Gently pat dry your silken tofu with a paper towel and cut into 6 equal pieces. In a medium bowl, combine the cornstarch, black pepper, white pepper, Chinese five-spice powder and salt.

Make the spice mixture: In a small bowl, stir together all the spice ingredients and set aside until needed.

Fry the tofu: In a wok, heat the vegetable oil over high heat until the surface begins to shimmer. Lightly coat the tofu pieces with the cornstarch mixture and, using a slotted spoon, carefully lower into the hot oil. Deep-fry the tofu for about 4 minutes, or until lightly browned and crisp. Remove from the wok with your slotted spoon, drain well on paper towels and sprinkle immediately with the spice mixture. Serve with Roasted Sichuan Chile Oil.

PANFRIED RADISH CAKE

The word for radish in Chinese sounds similar to the word for good fortune, so no surprises that it's popular around Chinese New Year. Most don't wait a whole year for this opportunity, though—you'll see this being pumped out of the kitchen at any decent dim sum establishment on the regular.

Not overly complex, the steamed radish cake itself is quite plain at first—but it really sings after a good panfrying, and even tossing it with some XO Sauce (page 138).

Starchy, salty, textural. The ultimate comfort food!

SERVES 6

Radish Cake

2¼ lbs (1 kg) daikon radishes

1 tbsp (18 g) salt

5 dried shiitake mushrooms

¾ oz (20 g) dried shrimp

Vegetable oil, for frying and loaf pan

1 Chinese sausage, diced

1 shallot, diced

2 green onions, chopped

2 cups minus 2 tbsp (300 g) white rice flour

Pinch of salt

Pinch of ground white pepper

Pinch of superfine sugar

Roasted Sichuan Chile Oil (page 130), for serving

Sliced green onion, for garnish

Prepare the radish: Peel and grate the radishes, using a box grater. Place in a large bowl and sprinkle with salt. Massage gently with your hands and set aside for about 20 minutes, or until soft.

In two separate bowls, soak the dried shiitake mushrooms and dried shrimp in hot water until softened. Squeeze the excess water from the mushrooms; remove and discard the stems and chop finely. Drain the shrimp well and finely chop.

Heat a wok over medium heat and add 2 tablespoons (30 ml) of vegetable oil. Add the shiitake mushrooms, shrimp, Chinese sausage and shallot. Cook, stirring constantly, for about 5 minutes, or until fragrant. Add the green onions and toss before removing from the heat. Let cool.

Squeeze the excess water from the radishes and reserve the liquid. In a medium bowl, combine the radish water with enough fresh water to make a total of 3⅓ cups (800 ml) of liquid, then stir the rice flour into this liquid until well incorporated. Stir the flour mixture back into the radish. Place a wok over medium heat, add this batter, stir and bring to a boil. Add the cooked mushroom mixture, salt, pepper and sugar and mix well to combine.

Pour the batter into a well-oiled loaf pan, place in a steamer and steam over medium-high heat for about 50 minutes. Remove from the steamer once cooked and let your radish cake set for about 30 minutes. Once cool, cut into ⅝-inch (1.5-cm)-thick slices.

Panfry the radish cake slices: In a large nonstick skillet, heat 2 tablespoons (30 ml) of vegetable oil over medium heat. Cook the radish cake slices until golden and crisp on both sides, about 6 minutes. Serve immediately with Roasted Sichuan Chile Oil and green onion.

FRIED SQUID TENTACLES

Fried squid tentacles, or deep-fried salt and pepper squid, is a solid favorite. Just like the Salt and Pepper Silken Tofu (page 116), this recipe uses the same salt and pepper mixture, with no batter!

The Chinese five-spice powder in the "dusting mix" imbues the squid with subtle notes of aniseed, spice and sweetness. Firm squid, in a starchy crispy shell, seasoned with lots of salt, garlic, green onion and chile. Yum!

If you're not a squid fan, worry not—everything tastes better deep-fried.

SERVES 4

1½ lbs (680 g) squid tentacles

1 tbsp (15 ml) Shaoxing rice wine

½ tsp sesame oil

Vegetable oil, for frying

Scant 2 tbsp (15 g) finely grated ginger

5 cloves garlic, sliced

2 long green chiles, sliced

1 long red chile, sliced

1 green onion, sliced

Flour Mixture

½ cup (60 g) all-purpose flour

½ cup (84 g) semolina

⅓ cup (58 g) polenta

1 tsp salt, plus more to season

½ tsp ground white pepper, plus more to season

Prepare the squid tentacles: In a medium bowl, combine the squid tentacles with the Shaoxing rice wine and sesame oil. Cover with plastic wrap and place in the fridge to marinate for at least 20 minutes.

Make the flour mixture: In a large bowl, stir together the flour, semolina, polenta, salt and white pepper.

Fill a wok half full with the vegetable oil. Heat over high heat until the surface begins to shimmer. Remove the squid from the fridge, dredge with the flour mixture and, working in batches, deep-fry until golden brown, 2 to 3 minutes. Drain and season immediately with extra salt and white pepper to taste.

Lower your wok to medium-high heat and add 1 tablespoon (15 ml) of vegetable oil. Add the ginger, garlic, green and red chiles and green onion and stir-fry for 30 seconds, or until aromatic. Add back the squid and toss gently to combine and infuse all the flavors. Serve immediately.

GRILLED FIVE-SPICE STEAK JIANBING

Jianbing is one of China's most-loved street snacks, and more than 2,000 years old! The crepelike pancake is typically made from mung bean flour and packed full of delicious savory fillings as well as wrapped in a crispy wonton wrapper. My contemporary twist is similar to a rice paper roll in concept, but uses an egg-based "wrap" instead of rice paper, for a very different flavor profile.

This recipe is a play on the traditional Peking duck pancake. The flank steak is marinated in a quick Chinese five-spice powder rub and then grilled. The steak is thinly sliced across the grain and served rolled in the jianbing with hoisin sauce, fresh cucumber slices and green onion . . . and some homemade roasted chile oil, if you're brave.

SERVES 4

Jianbing Batter

⅓ cup (53 g) millet flour

⅓ cup (40 g) all-purpose flour

1 tsp cornstarch

Pinch of salt

¾ cup + 2 tsp (190 ml) water

Five-Spice Steak

1 tsp Chinese five-spice powder

1 tsp light brown sugar

¾ tsp salt

Pinch of freshly ground black pepper

1 lb (450 g) flank steak

4 tsp (20 ml) vegetable oil

Vegetable oil, for pan

4 large eggs, beaten, divided

2 green onions, finely chopped

⅔ cup (160 ml) hoisin sauce, divided

½ cucumber, seeded and julienned

2 green onions, julienned

1 small carrot, peeled and julienned

Make the jianbing batter: In a medium bowl, combine all the batter ingredients and whisk until smooth and the batter is the consistency of heavy cream. Add 1 teaspoon of water at a time to thin the batter if necessary. Set aside until required.

Prepare the steak: In a small bowl, combine the Chinese five-spice powder, brown sugar, salt and ground black pepper. Rub the spice mixture over both sides of the flank steak.

Cook the steak: Heat a large skillet over medium-high heat. Add the vegetable oil to the pan and swirl to coat. Add the steak and cook for 4 minutes on each side for medium doneness, or until it reaches your desired doneness. Remove the steak from the pan and let stand, covered, for 5 to 10 minutes, then cut the steak across the grain into thin slices.

Cook the jianbing: Heat a large nonstick skillet over medium-high heat and brush with vegetable oil. When the oil begins to shimmer, pour in one-quarter of the jianbing batter. Working quickly, swirl the pan to spread the batter as thinly as possible. Cook the crepe for 1 to 2 minutes, or until firm. Pour ⅓ cup (80 ml) of the beaten eggs over the crepe, spread quickly and evenly with a spatula, sprinkle with a little chopped green onion and cook for 1 to 2 minutes until the egg is set.

Flip the crepe and spread the top side with 1 tablespoon (15 ml) of the hoisin sauce and continue to cook for another minute. Place a few slices of steak in the center along with some cucumber, julienned green onion and carrot. Fold in half twice and transfer to a platter. Repeat with the remaining ingredients. Serve immediately.

GRANDMÈRE'S BOXING CHICKEN

If you like chicken, but hate all the bones, this is such a nifty and delicious way to turn chicken wings into little lollipop drumsticks. This recipe maximizes meat, minimizes bone and is passed down from my Grandmère herself!

Like the Fried Squid Tentacles (page 120), the combination of flours gives a different and distinctive crunch that you normally only get from battering. Instead of using egg, the soy- and sesame-based marinade binds the crust to the lollipops by itself, so this recipe could easily welcome a vegan meat substitute.

Chicken wings like you've never had them before!

SERVES 4

Boxing Chicken

10 chicken wings

Vegetable oil, for deep-frying

Marinade

1 tbsp (15 ml) soy sauce

2 tsp (12 g) salt

2 tsp (9 g) superfine sugar

1 tsp sesame oil

½ tsp Chinese five-spice powder

1 tsp minced fresh ginger

1 tsp minced garlic

Flour Mixture

1 cup (130 g) cornstarch

¼ cup (30 g) all-purpose flour

2 tbsp (20 g) white rice flour

Pinch of salt

Sweet-and-Sour Sauce (page 134), for serving

Prepare the chicken: Cut off the wing tips and halve at the joints. Use a small knife to scrape the meat down the bones of each drumette to make a lollipop. Repeat this process with the wing pieces and remove the thinner bone.

In a medium bowl, combine the chicken lollipops with all the ingredients for the marinade and mix to coat well. Cover with plastic wrap and refrigerate for at least 3 hours to marinate.

When you're ready to cook the chicken, pour the oil into a deep saucepan until it is one-third full. Place the pan over high heat until the oil is 350°F (180°C). Test by dipping a wooden chopstick into the oil: The chopstick will cause the oil to sizzle when it's ready.

Make the flour mixture: In a medium bowl, stir together all the ingredients for the flour mixture and coat each chicken lollipop before gently lowering into the oil. Cook until golden brown, 3 to 5 minutes. Drain on a plate lined with paper towels and serve immediately with Sweet-and-Sour Sauce.

TEA-SMOKED DUCK BREAST

Smoking is a supereasy way to add another dimension to any meat. Instead of using different woods, tea leaves do all the work! You can use a delicate blend, such as jasmine tea, for subtler fragrant flavors, but something a bit heavier, such as black tea, really stands up to the richness of duck meat. Use whatever tea you have on hand, though!

You'll need to render and brown off the duck meat first, then it's as easy as chucking it in the smoker, putting on a pot of tea and coming back to it later!

Don't be overwhelmed if you haven't tried smoking meat before—as with most of the recipes in this book, all you really need is a wok!

SERVES 4

Spice Mixture

2 tbsp (36 g) salt

1½ tbsp (8 g) Sichuan peppercorns, toasted

2 tsp (3 g) black peppercorns, toasted

4 duck breasts, skin on

2 tbsp (30 ml) Shaoxing rice wine

Smoke Mixture

½ cup (98 g) uncooked white rice

½ cup (48 g) loose-leaf black tea

⅓ cup (75 g) packed light brown sugar

1 cinnamon stick

1 star anise pod

1 tsp dried orange peel (optional)

2 tbsp (30 ml) vegetable oil

Make the spice mixture: In a mortar and pestle, combine the salt, Sichuan peppercorns and black peppercorns and grind to form a fine powder. Brush the duck breasts with Shaoxing rice wine and coat evenly with the spice mixture. Wrap the duck breasts individually with plastic wrap and refrigerate to cure for at least 3 hours, preferably overnight. Once cured, rinse off each duck breast and pat dry with paper towels. Place, skin side up, on a wire rack and back into the fridge to dry out for at least 3 hours.

Prepare your wok by lining the inside with a double layer of aluminum foil, ensuring it is draped over the edges by enough of a margin to fold the excess upward later. Place all the ingredients for the smoke mixture in the bottom of the wok, followed by a wire rack. If you don't have a wire rack that fits, crisscross wooden skewers (soak them in water first) to create your own makeshift rack. Place the wok over high heat and once smoke begins to appear, lower the heat to medium. There will be lots of snapping and popping noises, but don't worry, this is normal. Place the duck breasts, skin side up, on the wire rack, cover with the lid of the wok and fold the aluminum foil over the lid, crimping to seal. Smoke the duck breasts for 25 minutes.

Remove the duck breasts from the wok and let cool. To finish, in a large skillet, heat the vegetable oil over medium-high heat and add the breasts, skin side down. Cook until the skin is gold and crisp, 4 to 6 minutes. Remove from the heat and slice across the grain. Serve warm.

SEVEN

DUMPLING SAUCES

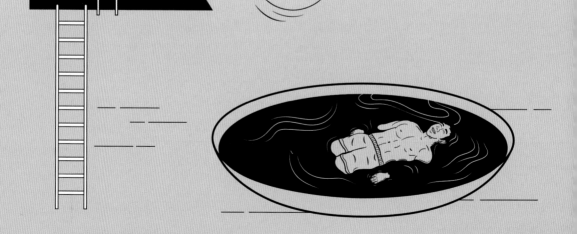

If you are like me, then you will need easy access to these sauces (hence why they are in a chapter on their own). Although this chapter is named "Dumpling Sauces," the sauces taste delicious on their own and complement most dishes, from fried rice to poached chicken to fresh salads. Make them in large batches and you will thank me later on.

Roasted Sichuan Chile Oil (page 130) is a must-have in our household. I use it in most dishes on the menu at Bumplings, and it's become so popular that we decided to jar it and sell it as is. The Bang Bang Sauce (page 137) is also a hit. It gives off the illusion of a delicious spicy and nutty Chilene satay sauce, however it does not use peanuts in any form so everyone can enjoy it.

ROASTED SICHUAN CHILE OIL

This is a must-have condiment in our family home, given it goes so well with almost anything. I even put it on my scrambled eggs in the morning to add a little punch. Don't forget: It keeps for a long time so make a large batch, although be wary—it won't last long!

MAKES 1 CUP (240 ML) OIL

- -

1 cup (240 ml) vegetable oil

1 cinnamon stick

3 star anise

2 tbsp (10 g) Sichuan peppercorns

2 bay leaves

¼ cup (14 g) crushed red pepper flakes

Pinch of salt

In a small saucepan, combine the vegetable oil, cinnamon, star anise, Sichuan peppercorns and bay leaves. Cook over low heat until the oil becomes fragrant, about 25 minutes. It is very easy to burn your spices at this point, so check in every now and then and adjust the heat as required.

Meanwhile, in a medium heatproof bowl, combine the red pepper flakes and salt. Once the oil mixture is fragrant, increase the heat to high and cook for an additional minute. Carefully strain the oil through a fine sieve into the bowl containing the red pepper flake mixture and stir well. The oil should sizzle and change color immediately. Let cool to room temperature before transferring to a jar to infuse further.

SICHUAN CHILE DRESSING

This sauce is so versatile. It is layered with different flavors—saltiness, tanginess, sweetness, a little spiciness and freshness from the cilantro. It's great with dumplings; however, the sauce can also be served as a salad dressing.

MAKES ¾ CUP (180 ML) SAUCE

- -

1 tbsp (5 g) crushed red pepper flakes

½ cup (120 ml) vegetable oil

2 tbsp (30 ml) tamari

4 tsp (20 ml) malt vinegar

1 tbsp (3 g) finely chopped fresh cilantro

2 tsp (9 g) superfine sugar

2 tbsp (30 ml) water

Place the red pepper flakes in a heatproof bowl. In a small saucepan, heat the oil over medium to high heat for 5 to 7 minutes. Carefully pour the hot oil over the red pepper flakes. Stir immediately and set aside, uncovered, letting it cool to room temperate to infuse, about 30 minutes. Once cool, strain the oil and stir in all the remaining ingredients.

BLACK VINEGAR AND TAMARI

This sauce is a favorite of mine and pairs perfectly with the Roasted Sichuan Chile Oil (page 130). When used in combination with our shrimp wontons (page 45), it creates a dish fit for kings. Make this a day in advance for the flavors to infuse. If you want to use it as a dressing, combine it with a little grapeseed oil before whisking to emulsify.

MAKES A SCANT ⅝ CUP (150 ML) SAUCE

---

5 tbsp (75 ml) Chinese black vinegar

¼ cup (60 ml) tamari

1 tbsp (13 g) superfine sugar

1 tsp sesame oil

1 medium clove garlic, minced

1 tbsp (6 g) minced green onion, white part only

In a small bowl, combine all the ingredients and stir until the sugar has dissolved. Cover and keep refrigerated until required.

SPICED VINEGAR SAUCE

Simple yet so complex, this vinegary spicy sauce helps transform a dish with its subtle hints of different spices. Again, eaten in combination with our Roasted Sichuan Chile Oil (page 130), the Spiced Vinegar Sauce will change a dish from being meh to mind-blowingly amazing!

MAKES ABOUT ⅞ CUP (210 ML) SAUCE

---

6 tbsp + 2 tsp (100 ml) Chinese black vinegar

6 tbsp + 2 tsp (100 ml) water

2 tsp (9 g) superfine sugar

1 small cinnamon stick

1 star anise

1 bay leaf

Pinch of fennel seeds

Pinch of Sichuan peppercorns

In a small nonreactive saucepan, combine all the ingredients and simmer over low heat until fragrant, about 5 minutes. Drain through a sieve into a bowl and discard the spices.

MUM'S FRIED GARLIC AND SOY

This is a condiment that reminds me so much of home. Grandmère makes it especially for wonton soup, but because there is always so much left over, we eat it for days on anything and everything.

MAKES ABOUT ¾ CUP (180 ML) SAUCE

¼ cup (60 ml) vegetable oil

4 medium cloves garlic, finely minced

½ cup (120 ml) soy sauce

1 long red chile, finely sliced

1 tsp sesame oil

In a small saucepan, heat the vegetable oil over medium-low heat. Add the minced garlic and cook, stirring, if necessary, to prevent the edges from browning too much, until fragrant and golden, about 5 minutes. Remove from the heat and transfer to a small bowl. Mix in the remaining ingredients.

SWEET-AND-SOUR SAUCE

This is a must-have in your repertoire if you are planning to embark on a Chinese culinary journey in your kitchen. Our Sweet-and-Sour Sauce is not only great for dipping, but can be served with most proteins and/or deep-fried food. Yum!

MAKES ABOUT 1 CUP (240 ML) SAUCE

¼ cup (60 g) packed light brown sugar

4 tsp (20 ml) ketchup

4 tsp (20 ml) soy sauce

¼ cup (60 ml) cider vinegar

Pinch of salt

½ cup (120 ml) water

2 tsp (5 g) cornstarch, dissolved in 2 tbsp (30 ml) water

In a small nonreactive saucepan, combine the brown sugar, ketchup, soy sauce, vinegar, salt and the water. Bring to a near boil over medium heat, stirring occasionally to dissolve the sugar. Give the cornstarch slurry a stir and add it to the pan. Continue to cook, stirring, for about 15 seconds, or until the sauce comes to full boil and thickens. Remove from the heat, transfer to a serving bowl and set aside for 10 minutes. Taste and season with more salt, if needed.

BANG BANG SAUCE

This is a Bumpling's signature sauce and a definite crowd-pleaser. Customers will often comment on the creamy nutty flavor and are often surprised by the lack of peanuts. Best made with our Roasted Sichuan Chile Oil (page 130), you can also make this dish with store-bought chile oil.

MAKES ABOUT 1¼ CUPS (300 ML) SAUCE

---

2 tbsp (30 ml) Chinese sesame paste or tahini

3 tbsp (45 ml) light soy sauce

2 tbsp (30 ml) Chinese black vinegar

2 tsp (9 g) superfine sugar

Pinch of Chinese five-spice powder

½ cup (120 ml) Roasted Sichuan Chile Oil (page 130)

2 cloves garlic, minced

¼ cup (60 ml) chicken broth or stock

In a medium bowl, combine all the ingredients and whisk until well mixed.

Before using, you can thin out the sauce with additional chicken broth, if desired.

GINGER-SOY STICKY SAUCE

Similar to the Sweet-and-Sour Sauce (page 134) the Ginger-Soy Sticky Sauce exudes sweet and savory stickiness that goes so well with any kind of meat. I love this so much I would even eat it with plain steamed rice.

MAKES ABOUT 1¼ CUPS (300 ML) SAUCE

---

1 cup + 2 tsp (250 ml) tamari or reduced-salt soy sauce

1 cup + 2 tsp (250 ml) pineapple juice

¼ cup + scant 3 tbsp (100 g) packed light brown sugar

½ cup + 2 tbsp (150 ml) honey

4 cloves garlic, minced

5 tbsp (40 g) finely grated fresh ginger

In a medium saucepan, combine all the ingredients and bring to a boil. Reduce the heat to low and simmer for about 20 minutes, stirring occasionally. Once the sauce has reduced by half and coats the back of a spoon, it is ready. Strain through a sieve and into a bowl. The sauce will thicken further as it cools. Before using, you can thin out the sauce with additional pineapple juice, if desired.

NOTE

I find strained pineapple juice from canned pineapple works best for this sauce.

XO SAUCE

All chefs have their own version of XO sauce that they guard with their life. I'm not about that! I think this sauce is so delicious, it would be wrong of me not to share it.

MAKES ABOUT 2 CUPS (480 ML) SAUCE

----

2 oz (60 g) dried scallops

2 oz (60 g) dried shrimp

1 cup (240 ml) just-boiled water, divided

1 cup (240 ml) vegetable oil, divided

6 large cloves garlic, finely chopped

2 shallots, finely chopped

2 oz (60 g) prosciutto, finely shredded

6 long red chiles, seeded and finely chopped

3 dried long red chiles, seeded, soaked and finely chopped

1 tbsp (13 g) superfine sugar, or to taste

Pinch of salt

Soak the dried scallops and dried shrimp separately in ½ cup (120 ml) of hot water each for about 3 hours or overnight if possible. Drain and reserve the soaking water from both. Finely shred the scallops and finely chop the shrimp.

In a wok, heat half of the vegetable oil over medium-high heat and add the scallops. Cook until crisp, about 2 minutes. Remove with a strainer, leaving the oil in the wok, and set them aside.

Add the remaining oil to the wok and lower to medium heat. Add the garlic, shallots and chopped shrimp and cook, stirring constantly, until golden brown, about 5 minutes. Add the prosciutto and the fresh and dried chiles and cook for 30 seconds. Add the scallops and reserved soaking water. Cook, stirring constantly, for an additional 30 seconds. Add the sugar and salt and cook until the water has evaporated and the sauce is fragrant, about 30 minutes, making sure to stir occasionally. Remove from the heat and transfer to a jar. Store in the refrigerator.

EIGHT

DUMPLING WRAPPERS

WONTON WRAPPERS

MAKES 36 WRAPPERS

----

2 cups (250 g) all-purpose flour, plus more for dusting

Pinch of salt

1 large egg, lightly beaten

6 tbsp (90 ml) water

Cornstarch, for dusting

In a large bowl, stir together the flour and salt. Create a well in the center and slowly pour in the egg and water while mixing with a pair of chopsticks. If there is still dry flour in your bowl, add 1 tablespoon (15 ml) of water at a time and continue to mix until a pliable dough is formed. Turn out onto a lightly floured surface and knead your dough until elastic, 5 to 10 minutes. Cover with a damp tea towel and set aside to rest for 30 minutes.

Cut the dough into 4 equal pieces. Dust a clean work surface with cornstarch and roll each piece out very thinly into an 11-inch (28-cm) square. You can use a knife to trim the edges. Cut each square into 9 equal smaller squares. Cover with a clean, damp tea towel to prevent it from drying out.

CRYSTAL DUMPLING WRAPPERS

MAKES 30 WRAPPERS

----

1 cup (125 g) wheat starch

½ cup (63 g) tapioca starch

Pinch of salt

1 cup + 2 tsp (250 ml) boiling water

4 tsp (20 ml) canola oil

In a large bowl, stir together the wheat starch, tapioca starch and salt. Create a well in the center and, working quickly, pour in the boiling water while mixing with a wooden spoon. The dough will start off looking translucent before becoming white and lumpy. Once the water has been incorporated, stir in the oil. The key here is to achieve a medium to firm texture, so if the dough is mushy, work in extra wheat starch, 1 tablespoon (8 g) at a time. Similarly, if the dough is too dry, add a little extra water. Turn the dough out onto an unfloured surface and knead until smooth, 3 to 5 minutes. The texture should resemble that of Play-Doh. Cut the dough into 4 equal pieces, seal well in a ziplock bag and set aside to rest for 5 minutes.

Once rested, form 1 piece of dough into a long log and cut into 6 portions of similar weight. Working with 1 portion at a time, press flat with the palm of your hand to form a round disk. Using a rolling pin, roll into a round wrapper 3½ to 4 inches (9 to 10 cm) in diameter. Use immediately.

NOTE

Wheat starch is a fine, gluten-free starch used in Chinese cuisine.

DUMPLING WRAPPERS

- -

2 cups (250 g) all-purpose flour, plus more for dusting

Pinch of salt

½ cup + 2 tbsp (150 ml) water

In a large bowl, stir together the flour and salt. Create a well in the center and slowly pour in the water while mixing with a pair of chopsticks. If there is still dry flour in your bowl, add 1 tablespoon (15 ml) of water at a time and continue to mix until a pliable dough is formed. Turn onto a lightly floured surface and knead your dough until elastic, 15 to 20 minutes (you can use a mixer to do this job for you). Cover with a damp tea towel and set aside to rest for 30 minutes.

Once rested, reknead your dough on a lightly floured surface for 5 minutes, then roll into a long log. Cut the log into 24 portions of similar weight. Then, working with 1 portion of dough at a time, press flat with the palm of your hand to form a round disk. Using a rolling pin, roll into a round wrapper that's 1 millimeter thick and 3½ to 4 inches (9 to 10 cm) in diameter. It's okay if the wrapper is not perfectly round. Repeat the process to form the remaining wrappers, then cover with a clean, damp tea towel to prevent them from drying out.

RAINBOW DUMPLING WRAPPERS

- -

2¼ cups (285 g) all-purpose flour, plus more for dusting

1 tsp salt

½ cup (120 ml) boiling water

¼ cup (60 ml) colored puree (see chapter 4)

In a large bowl, stir together the flour and salt. Create a well in the center and slowly pour in the water and colored puree while mixing with a pair of chopsticks. If there is still dry flour in your bowl, add 1 tablespoon (15 ml) of water at a time and continue to mix until a pliable dough is formed. Turn out onto a lightly floured surface and knead your dough until elastic, 15 to 20 minutes (you can use a mixer to do this job for you). Cover with a clean, damp tea towel and set aside to rest for 30 minutes.

Once rested, reknead your dough on a lightly floured surface for 5 minutes, then roll into a long log. Cut the log into 24 portions of similar weight. Then, working with 1 portion of dough at a time, press flat with the palm of your hand to form a round disk. Using a rolling pin, roll into a round wrapper that's 1 millimeter thick and 3½ to 4 inches (9 to 10 cm) in diameter. It's okay if the wrapper is not perfectly round. Repeat the process to form the remaining wrappers, then cover with a clean, damp tea towel to prevent them from drying out.

NINE

DUMPLING FOLDS AND SHAPES

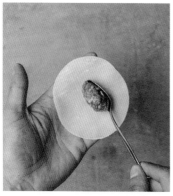

TRIANGLE SHAPE

Folding dumplings for the first time can seem like a scary task. To help ease into it, I thought I'd start with a simple one—the triangle fold.

1. Working with 1 dumpling wrapper at a time, place a teaspoon of filling in the center.

2. Pinch one end of the wrapper along two edges and seal the dumpling about one-third of the way to the middle.

3. Using your index finger, push the open side of the wrapper toward the center to make a triangle shape.

4. Pinch the seams to make sure your dumpling is well sealed.

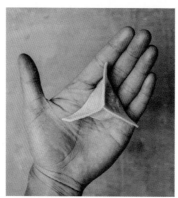

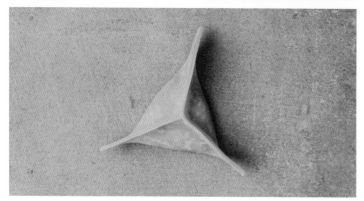

THE SIMPLE POTSTICKER

Another easy fold, the simple pot-sticker is perfect for a panfried dumpling. With a shape like this one, you can fit many dumplings into your pan by aligning them in a grid formation.

1. Working with 1 dumpling wrapper at a time, place a teaspoon of filling in the center.

2. Fold into a taco shape and, bringing two opposite ends together, pinch to seal at the top.

3. Using your index finger, push the rounded open edge up to meet the sealed pointed end, then press to seal.

4. Repeat this on the other side.

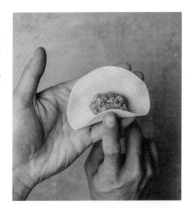
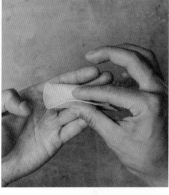

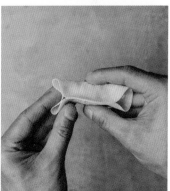
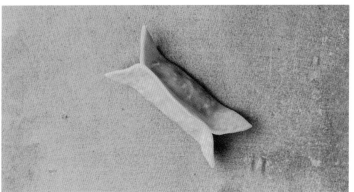

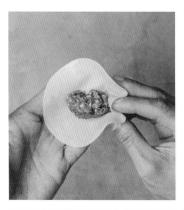

HALF-MOON

One of the most versatile dumpling shapes, the half-moon can be cooked in various ways.

1. Working with 1 dumpling wrapper at a time, place a teaspoon of filling in the center. Fold into a taco shape.

2. Use your thumb, index and middle fingers to make a W-shape at one end of the folded dumpling and press together to seal.

3. Pinch the folded dumpling skin together until you reach the halfway point of the seam.

4. Repeat the W formation on the open side and pinch to seal it.

5. Take your half-moon dumpling and pull the edges to give it a slight curve.

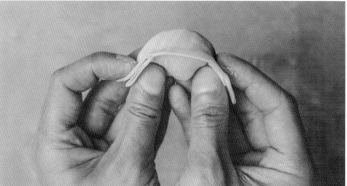

CRESCENT MOON

This fold will test your skill as a dumpling master. If you can accomplish 7 pleats, then you can call yourself a pro; 10 pleats, and you can open your very own restaurant.

1. Working with 1 dumpling wrapper at a time, place a tablespoon (15 g) of filling in the center.

2. Hold the wrapper slightly cupped in your hand and fold over into a half-moon shape without pinching to seal.

3. Using your free hand, make a small pleat on the side of the wrapper closest to you by pinching the edge firmly.

4. Continue to make pleats while moving along the side of the wrapper, until you create a crescent shape and the dumpling is completely sealed.

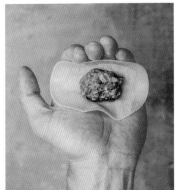
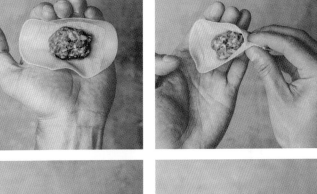

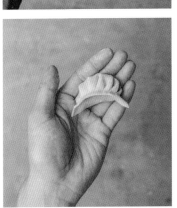

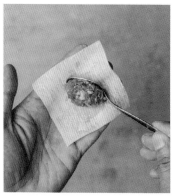
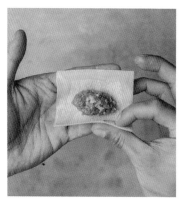

CLASSIC WONTON FOLD

This dumpling fold was the first I learned and was taught to me by my Grandmère. I have also passed this skill on to my little brothers. It is elegant in looks and perfect for boiling and/or deep-frying.

1. Working with 1 wonton wrapper at a time, place a teaspoon of filling in the center.

2. Brush half of the edges of the square with water.

3. Fold the wet edges over in half to make a rectangular shape and enclose the filling.

4. Brush one of the corners with water and fold inward to overlap with the other corner.

5. Press to seal.

GOLD INGOT SHAPE

This dumpling shape is considered a symbol of good fortune, resembling the shape of an ancient Chinese gold ingot. Its functionality also serves as a purpose for holding sauce. This shape is easy to make—my seven-year-old brother has perfected it!

1. Working with 1 dumpling wrapper at a time, place a teaspoon of filling in the center. Brush half of the perimeter with water.

2. Fold the wet edge over to meet the dry edge, to form a semicircle.

3. Pinch along the edge to seal and enclose the filling.

4. Brush one corner of your semicircle with water and fold inward to overlap with the other corner.

5. Press to seal.

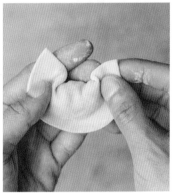

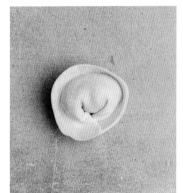

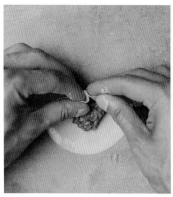
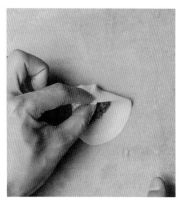

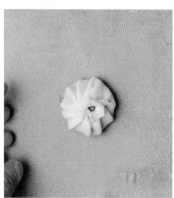

SOUP DUMPLING SHAPE

There is no doubt this is the most challenging of the folds, which is why I kept it for last. Master the other folds first, and you will no doubt be able to make this one, too. I recommend starting with a little less filling to begin with while you get used to perfecting this shape.

1. Working with 1 dumpling wrapper at a time, place 1 tablespoon (15 g) of filling in the center.

2. Place the wrapper flat onto a working surface and, using both sets of your index fingers and thumbs, pinch the edge firmly to fold a pleat.

3. Continue this until you have formed pleats along the entire edge of the wrapper.

4. Pinch and twist the dough at the end to ensure it is completely enclosed and sealed.

ACKNOWLEDGMENTS

First, thank you to all my cousins, aunties, uncles and other extended family members who have helped me with this book—even if it's just helping me out with running Bumplings so I could make this possible.

Mum (Dany)—You are the most important person to mention here. It's not just the cooking, but also the encouragement and giving me the confidence to do the things I didn't think I could do. Also, thanks for being on my back about writing all my recipes down—I regretted not having done this a few times while writing this book.

Grandmère (Josephine)—Thank you for always being so excited about food and being so welcoming to teaching others. You've been my biggest inspiration in the kitchen—starting with wontons, then dim sum, then learning how to catch, fillet and cook a fish!

To my younger brothers (Brad, Liam and Josh), thanks for letting me practice my recipes on you.

Brad—I can't thank you enough for all the help you've given me in getting Bumplings off the ground. You're the best.

Pete—Not only a father figure, but always so supportive of me in all of my business endeavors. Thanks, Pete.

Dad (Richard)—There's only one person who loves deep-fried Asian food as much as me, and it's got to be you. Thanks for keeping me greasy and for phoning me every morning at seven a.m.

Nick—None of this would have been possible without my best friend and partner, Nick. You have stood by me during every struggle and helped celebrate all my successes. I am forever grateful for your love and patience. This is me letting the rest of the world know they have this book because of you.

ABOUT THE AUTHOR

Brendan Pang is an Australian cook, born and raised in Perth, recognized in his home country for his proficiency in dumplings and contemporary Asian cuisine.

Born into a Mauritian-Chinese family, he has had vast exposure to a diverse cultural upbringing and flavors that arise from this unique upbringing in Australia.

The art of making dumplings and many of the recipes in this book were passed down from his Grandmère, who first taught him to make wontons during school holidays when he was nine years old. Grandmère taught Brendan not only how to cook food, but that sharing it with those you love makes it even sweeter. But his true passion, drive and love of experimentation is testament to his mother, Dany. Despite exposure to dumplings from a young age, many traditional Chinese dishes and regular dim sum with the family, no one was ever able to make his dim sum favorites (e.g., har gow, siu mai, char siu bao)—this was a turning point for Brendan to learn how!

After he graduated in 2016 from Curtin University and worked as a social worker in the north of regional Western Australia (Broome), Brendan's passion for food and expression of his cultural heritage became his major driver, overtaking his career focus and leading him to build his food empire!

Since then, Brendan has starred on the Network 10 TV show *MasterChef Australia*, which has helped him expand his mastery into other culinary techniques and cuisines. Not only has Brendan mastered the art of making dumplings, dim sum favorites and classic Chinese cuisine, but he has recently opened his own catering–restaurant–traveling food concept: Bumplings. In addition to serving up his grade-A dumplings, he regularly teaches dumpling master classes.

INDEX

A

aioli, 84
appetizers/snacks
    Chinese Pickled Radish, 108
    Fried Squid Tentacles, 120
    Grandmère's Boxing Chicken, 124
    Green Onion Pancake, 115
    Grilled Five-Spice Steak Jianbing, 123
    Panfried Radish Cake, 119
    Salt and Pepper Silken Tofu, 116
    Sesame Shrimp Toasts, 112
    Smacked Cucumber Salad, 111
    Tea-Smoked Duck Breast, 127

B

bacon, Chinese, 95
bamboo shoots, 15
Bang Bang Sauce, 137
bao
    BBQ Pork Steamed Buns, 91
    Fried Chicken Bao Buns, 84–86
    Juicy Chicken Sheng Jian Bao, 48
    Pork, Carrot and Ginger Baozi, 73
    Pork and Garlic Chive Baozi, 92
Bao Bun Dough, 86
baozi. See bao
BBQ pork, Chinese, 59, 91, 103
BBQ Pork and Crispy Wonton Noodles, 103
BBQ Pork Steamed Buns, 91
bean sprouts
    Cantonese Chicken and Salted Fish Fried Rice, 100
    Classic Chinese Fried Rice, 96
    Korean Beef Dumplings, 67–68
beef, ground
    Beef Dumplings in Hot and Sour Soup, 42
    Chinese Spicy Beef Potstickers, 55
    Curried Beef Dumplings, 74
    Korean Beef Dumplings, 67–68
Beef Dumplings in Hot and Sour Soup, 42
beets, 67–68, 69–70
Biang Biang Noodles with Spicy Cumin Lamb, 87–88

Black Cod and Chive Dumplings, 81
black fungus, 16
black vinegar, Chinese
    Black Vinegar and Tamari, 133
    Shanghai Soup Dumplings, 23
    Spiced Vinegar Sauce, 133
Black Vinegar and Tamari, 133
black wrappers, 81
blue wrappers, 77
bok choy
    Biang Biang Noodles with Spicy Cumin Lamb, 87–88
    Cantonese-Style Shrimp Wonton Soup, 45
    Red Curry Chicken Wonton Soup, 41
Boxing chicken, 124
broth, pork bone, 45
buns. See bao

C

cabbage
    Chile Mud Crab Dumplings, 77
    Juicy Chicken Sheng Jian Bao, 48

Miso Roasted Eggplant
Potstickers, 78
Panfried Chicken and
Cabbage
Dumplings, 51
Tofu and Kimchi Jiaozi, 27
Cantonese Chicken and Salted
Fish Fried Rice, 100
Cantonese-Style Shrimp Wonton
Soup, 45
carrots
Grilled Five-Spice Steak
Jianbing, 123
pickled for Fried Chicken Bao
Buns, 84
Pork, Carrot and Ginger
Baozi, 73
Red Curry Chicken Wonton
Soup, 41
Tofu and Kimchi Jiaozi, 27
celery
Beef Dumplings in Hot and
Sour Soup, 42
Chinese Spicy Beef
Potstickers, 55
pickled, for Lobster XO
Dumplings, 37
char slu (Chinese BBQ pork), 91,
103
chicken. See also chicken,
ground
Cantonese Chicken and
Salted Fish Fried
Rice, 100
Chicken and Cilantro
Dumplings, 64

Fried Chicken Bao Buns,
84–86
Grandmère's Boxing Chicken,
124
Juicy Chicken Sheng Jian
Bao, 48
Sticky Rice Wrapped in Lotus
Leaf, 95
chicken, ground. See also
chicken
Chicken and Ginger Jiaozi, 33
Panfried Chicken and
Cabbage
Dumplings, 51
Red Curry Chicken Wonton
Soup, 41
Chicken and Cilantro Dumplings,
64
Chicken and Ginger Jiaozi, 33
Chile and Garlic Dipping Sauce,
99
Chile Mud Crab Dumplings, 77
chiles
green, 103, 120
red, 108, 120, 134, 138
red bird's eye, 99
Chinese bacon, 95
Chinese BBQ pork, 59, 91, 103
Chinese black vinegar, 23, 133
Chinese Pickled Radish, 108
Chinese Roast Duck Dumplings,
69–70
Chinese sausage, 95, 96, 119
Chinese Spicy Beef Potstickers,
55
chives, garlic, 34, 92

choy sum, 103, 104
cilantro
Beef Dumplings in Hot and
Sour Soup, 42
Biang Biang Noodles with
Spicy Cumin Lamb,
87–88
Chicken and Cilantro
Dumplings, 64
Pork and Peanut Dumplings,
20
cinnamon
Spiced Vinegar Sauce, 133
Roasted Sichuan Chile Oil,
130
Tea-Smoked Duck Breast,
127
Classic Chinese Fried Rice, 96
cod, black, 81
colored wrappers. See wrappers
cong you bing (Green Onion
Pancake), 115
corn, 42, 55
crabmeat, 77, 99
Cranberry and Pinot Noir Sauce,
69–70
crepe, 123
crescent moon fold, 147
Crispy Taro Dumplings, 60
crusting
Fried Squid Tentacles, 120
Grandmère's Boxing Chicken,
124
Salt and Pepper Silken Tofu,
116
Crystal Dumpling Wrappers, 141

Crystal Shrimp Har Gow, 15
Cucumber Salad Dressing, 111
cucumbers, 111, 123
cumin, 24, 87–88
Curried Beef Dumplings, 74
curry, 41, 74

D

daikon radishes, 108, 119
Dan Dan Sauce, 104
dough, 60, 86
dressings, 111, 130
duck
    Chinese Roast Duck
        Dumplings, 69–70
    Tea-Smoked Duck Breast,
        127
Dumpling Wrappers, 142

E

eggplants, 78

F

fish. See also seafood
    black cod, 81
    salted, 100
    white, 37
folds. See shapes/folds
Fried BBQ Pork Dumplings, 59
Fried Chicken Bao Buns, 84–86
fried rice
    Cantonese chicken and
        salted fish, 100
    classic Chinese, 96
    special crab, 99
Fried Squid Tentacles, 120

G

garlic chives, 34, 92
ginger
    Cantonese-Style Shrimp
        Wonton Soup, 45
    Chicken and Cilantro
        Dumplings, 64
    Chicken and Ginger Jiaozi, 33
    Ginger Vinegar Sauce, 23
    Ginger-Soy Sticky Sauce, 137
    Northern-Style Lamb
        Dumplings, 24
    Pork, Carrot and Ginger
        Baozi, 73
    Pork and Peanut Dumplings,
        20
    Scallop and Ginger
        Dumplings, 19
    Special Crab Fried Rice, 99
    Swiss Chard and Spinach
        Jiaozi, 16
    Tofu and Kimchi Jiaozi, 27
Ginger Vinegar Sauce, 23
Ginger-Soy Sticky Sauce, 137
Gochujang Aioli, 84
gold ingot, dumpling shape, 149
Grandmère's Boxing Chicken,
    124
Grandmère's Fried Shrimp
    Wontons, 56
green chiles, 103, 120
green dumplings, 64
Green Onion Pancake, 115
greens
    bok choy, 41, 45, 87–88
    cabbage (see cabbage)

    choy sum, 103, 104
    kang kung, 38
    mustard, 99, 104
    spinach, 16, 64
    Swiss chard, 16
Grilled Five-Spice Steak Jianbing,
    123
ground beef. See beef, ground

H

half-moon, dumpling shape, 146
har gow, 15

J

jianbing, 123
jiaozi
    chicken and ginger, 33
    pork and garlic chive, 34
    Swiss chard and spinach, 16
    tofu and kimchi, 27
Juicy Chicken Sheng Jian Bao,
    48

K

Kang Kung and Tofu Dumplings,
    38
kimchi
    Korean Beef Dumplings, 67–
        68
    Panfried Pork and Kimchi
        Dumplings, 52
    Tofu and Kimchi Jiaozi, 27
Korean Beef Dumplings, 67–68

L

lamb
    Biang Biang Noodles with
        Spicy Cumin Lamb,
        87–88
    Northern-Style Lamb
        Dumplings, 24
lap cheong (Chinese sausage),
    95, 96, 119
lap yuk (Chinese bacon), 95
Lobster XO Dumplings, 37
lotus leaves, 95

M

mandu (Korean dumplings), 52,
    67–68
marinade, 124
mayonnaise, 84
Miso Roasted Eggplant
    Potstickers, 78
mud crab, 77
Mum's Fried Garlic and Soy, 134
mung bean sprouts
    Cantonese Chicken and
        Salted Fish Fried
        Rice, 100
    Classic Chinese Fried Rice, 96
    Korean Beef Dumplings, 67–
        68
mushrooms. See shiitake
    mushrooms
mustard greens, 99, 104

N

napa cabbage. See cabbage
noodles
    BBQ Pork and Crispy Wonton
        Noodles, 103
    Biang Biang Noodles with
        Spicy Cumin Lamb,
        87–88
    Korean Beef Dumplings, 67–
        68
    Spicy Dan Dan Noodles, 104
Northern-Style Lamb Dumplings,
    24

O

oils. See also sauces
    fragrant cilantro, 64
    roasted Sichuan chile, 130
    shallot, 103
onion, green pancake, 115
orange wrappers, 73

P

palate cleanser, 108
Panfried Chicken and Cabbage
    Dumplings, 51
Panfried Pork and Kimchi
    Dumplings, 52
Panfried Radish Cake, 119
peanuts, 20
pepper, and salt silken tofu, 116
peppercorns, Sichuan
    Beef Dumplings in Hot and
        Sour Soup, 42
    Chinese Spicy Beef
        Potstickers, 55
    Curried Beef Dumplings, 74
    Northern-Style Lamb
        Dumplings, 24
    Roasted Sichuan Chile Oil,
        130

Tea-Smoked Duck Breast,
    127
pickled
    carrots, 84
    celery, 37
    green chiles, 103
    radishes, 108
pineapple juice, 137
pink wrappers, 69–70
Pinot noir, 69–70
pork. See also bacon, Chinese;
    pork, Chinese BBQ;
    sausages, Chinese
    Crispy Taro Dumplings, 60
    Panfried Pork and Kimchi
        Dumplings, 52
    Pork, Carrot and Ginger
        Baozi, 73
    Pork and Garlic Chive Baozi,
        92
    Pork and Garlic Chive Jiaozi,
        34
    Pork and Peanut Dumplings,
        20
    Pork and Shrimp Siu Mai, 12
    Shanghai Soup Dumplings,
        23
    Spicy Dan Dan Noodles, 104
    Spicy Sichuan Pork Wontons,
        30
Pork, Carrot and Ginger Baozi, 73
pork, Chinese BBQ, 59, 91, 103
Pork and Garlic Chive Baozi, 92
Pork and Garlic Chive Jiaozi, 34
Pork and Peanut Dumplings, 20
Pork and Shrimp Siu Mai, 12

pork chuck bones, 45

pork fat, 15

potstickers

    Chinese spicy beef, 55

    folding, 145

    Miso Roasted Eggplant
        Potstickers, 78

prosciutto, 138

purple wrappers, 78

R

radishes, 108, 119

Rainbow Dumpling Wrappers,
    142

red bird's eye chiles, 99

red chiles

    Chinese Pickled Radish, 108

    Fried Squid Tentacles, 120

    Mum's Fried Garlic and Soy,
        134

    XO Sauce, 138

Red Curry Chicken Wonton Soup,
    41

red dumplings, 67–68

red radishes, 108

rice

    Cantonese Chicken and
        Salted Fish Fried
        Rice, 100

    Classic Chinese Fried Rice, 96

    Special Crab Fried Rice, 99

    Sticky Rice Wrapped in Lotus
        Leaf, 95

    Tea-Smoked Duck Breast,
        127

Roasted Sichuan Chile Oil, 130

S

sablefish, 81

Salt and Pepper Silken Tofu, 116

salted fish, 100

samphire, 77

sauces. See also oils

    bang bang, 137

    for BBQ Pork and Crispy
        Wonton Noodles,
        103

    black vinegar and tamari, 133

    chile and garlic, 99

    cranberry and Pinot noir,
        69–70

    Dan Dan, 104

    ginger vinegar, 23

    ginger-soy sticky, 137

    spiced vinegar, 133

    sweet-and-sour, 134

    XO, 138

sausages, Chinese

    Classic Chinese Fried Rice, 96

    Panfried Radish Cake, 119

    Sticky Rice Wrapped in Lotus
        Leaf, 95

Scallop and Ginger Dumplings,
    19

scallops, 19, 138

seafood. See also fish

    lobster, 37

    scallops, 19, 138

    shrimp (see shrimp)

Sesame Shrimp Toasts, 112

Shallot Oil, 103

Shanghai Soup Dumplings, 23

shapes/folds

    classic wonton, 148

    crescent moon, 147

    gold ingot, 149

    half-moon, 146

    simple potsticker, 145

    soup dumpling, 150

    triangle, 144

sheng jian bao, 48

shiitake mushrooms

    Panfried Radish Cake, 119

    Pork and Peanut Dumplings,
        20

    Pork and Shrimp Siu Mai, 12

    Sticky Rice Wrapped in Lotus
        Leaf, 95

    Swiss Chard and Spinach
        Jiaozi, 16

shrimp

    Cantonese-Style Shrimp
        Wonton Soup, 45

    Classic Chinese Fried Rice, 96

    Crystal Shrimp Har Gow, 15

    Grandmère's Fried Shrimp
        Wontons, 56

    Pork and Shrimp Siu Mai, 12

    Sesame Shrimp Toasts, 112

Sichuan Chile Dressing, 130

Sichuan peppercorns. See
    peppercorns, Sichuan

silken tofu, 116

siu mai (open-topped dumplings),
    12

Smacked Cucumber Salad, 111

smoke mixture, 127

snacks/appetizers. See
    appetizers/snacks

soup dumplings, 23, 150
soups
    Beef Dumplings in Hot and
        Sour Soup, 42
    Cantonese-Style Shrimp
        Wonton Soup, 45
    Red Curry Chicken Wonton
        Soup, 41
Special Crab Fried Rice, 99
Spiced Vinegar Sauce, 133
Spicy Dan Dan Noodles, 104
Spicy Sichuan Pork Wontons, 30
spinach, 16, 64
spinach, water, 38
squid tentacles, 120
steak, 123
Sticky Rice Wrapped in Lotus
    Leaf, 95
sweet potato starch noodles,
    67–68
Sweet-and-Sour Sauce, 134
Swiss Chard and Spinach Jiaozi,
    16

T
tamari, 133, 137
Tara Dough, 60
Tea-Smoked Duck Breast, 127
tofu
    Kang Kung and Tofu
        Dumplings, 38
    Korean Beef Dumplings, 67–
        68
    Panfried Pork and Kimchi
        Dumplings, 52
    Tofu and Kimchi Jiaozi, 27

Tofu and Kimchi Jiaozi, 27
tomato sauce, 77
triangle fold, 144

V
vinegar, Chinese black
    Black Vinegar and Tamari,
        133
    Shanghai Soup Dumplings,
        23
    Spiced Vinegar Sauce, 133

W
water chestnuts, 16
watercress, 38
wine, red, 69–70
wings, chicken, 124
Wonton Wrappers, 141
wontons
    folding, 148
    Grandmère's fried shrimp, 56
    noodles, 103
    soup, 41, 45
    spicy Sichuan pork, 30
    wrappers, 141
wrappers
    black, 81
    blue, 77
    crystal dumpling, 141
    green, 64
    orange, 73
    pink, 69–70
    purple, 78
    rainbow dumpling, 142
    red, 67–68

wonton, 141
yellow, 74

X
xiao long bao (Shanghai soup
    dumplings), 23, 150
XO Sauce, 138

Y
yellow wrappers, 74